NANCIE
CARMICHAEL

Surviving
ONE
BAD
YEAR

7 Spiritual Strategies to
Lead You to a New Beginning

 **HOWARD BOOKS**
A DIVISION OF SIMON & SCHUSTER, INC.

New York Nashville London Toronto Sydney

Published by Howard Books, a division of Simon & Schuster, Inc.
1230 Avenue of the Americas, New York, NY 10020
www.howardpublishing.com

Surviving One Bad Year © 2009 Nancie Carmichael

Published in association with Credo Communications, LLC

Library of Congress Control Number: 2009014062

ISBN: 978-1-4391-0324-1

10   9   8   7   6   5   4   3   2   1

Manufactured in the United States of America

For information regarding special discounts for bulk purchases, please contact: Simon & Schuster Special Sales at 1-866-506-1949 or business@simonandschuster.com.

The Simon & Schuster Speakers Bureau can bring authors to your live event. For more information or to book an event contact the Simon & Schuster Speakers Bureau at 1-866-248-3049 or visit our website at www.simonspeakers.com.

Interior design by Davina Mock-Maniscalco

A special thanks to the many friends who shared their personal stories for the creation of this book. All stories are used by permission.

Contents

Acknowledgments

To Philis Boultinghouse, my editor: *Thank you for partnering with me to shape the message of this book. Your keen insight and skill have been invaluable!* I'm grateful as well for Miriam Mendez, professor at George Fox Evangelical Seminary, who gave important feedback at the very beginning of this book. I'm thankful, too, for David Sanford, my agent. And to my women's Bible study group: *What a journey we're all on! Each one of you means the world to me.*

One of the early church fathers said with a sigh, "The toil my writing cost me, the difficulties I underwent, how often I gave up in despair, and how I started again, both I who knew the burden, and those who lived with me can bear witness" (Jerome, 331–420 A.D.).

So, the biggest thanks go to "those who live with me." My kids and kids-in-law—Jon and Brittni; Eric and Carly; Chris and Jami; Andrew and Michelle; Amy and Jeff—*you are my heart!* Bill, my lifelong love and fellow adventurer—*I love you so!*

It's been said that names are seeds. For that reason, I list the names of precious seeds in my life, my grandchildren. Your Nana loves you with all her heart, and prays that your love for God and others will define each of your lives in unique ways. I already see it happening:

- *Will:* My thinking, wonderful grandson, you started it all, sending Papa and me on the best adventure yet! I love that you're a "bookworm" and that you care so much about people. We're so proud of you.

- *Kendsy:* I love that you walk along the Metolius River with me and see the wonderful things God makes. Keep writing and "noticing" life!
- *Cali:* I love your smile, your songs, and your creative heart. You are growing so fast and make us smile with the funny things you say.
- *Hogan:* Thank you for helping me feed the birds and for enjoying everything in life. I love to see how much you love your family.
- *Pearson:* It's so fun to watch your passion for "hoop" ball— even though you're just three (and I love that you have my maiden name)!
- *Jackson:* I love hearing your amazingly grown-up insights on life, now that you're *four.* (I'm so glad you like *Uncle Wiggily,* too!)
- *Cole*, my littlest baby grandson, just learning to walk: Your smile and zest for life is beautiful to see. (Don't grow up too fast!)
- *Wesley:* Thanks for your recipe for Wesley Eggs! And Papa and I love it that you want to lead worship when you're older.
- *Annabelle:* I love your graceful, feminine ways and your beautiful brown eyes. More than we can say, Papa and I are grateful for you!

But now abideth faith, hope, love, these three; and the greatest of these is love (1 Corinthians 13: 13).

INTRODUCTION

To You, My Friend

Tʜɪs ʙᴏᴏᴋ ɪs dedicated to you, my friend, in the midst of your impossible year—a year marked forever by an event that threatens to consume you. I have written out of my own experience and that of others to offer hope that you will survive and, indeed, thrive.

Our common thread is that we are walking through something we cannot control; and as much as we try, we don't see a pain-free or easy solution. We only know we have to get *through* it. You may have lost a family member to death; you may be facing a serious illness, a divorce, or financial reversal. Or perhaps your loss is difficult to define. Your life has simply hit a stall, and you are filled with a quiet desperation as you go through the motions. You feel stuck and wonder, *Is God there? Does He care about me? Surely there's more . . .*

As a friend suffering from brain cancer wrote me, "Everyone carries a bag of rocks. Some are bigger, some smaller." Some losses are certainly more traumatic and life-altering than others, but loss is loss. Trouble is trouble. Pain is pain.

Life can wear us down, and sometimes we're tempted to give up. Our dreams recede, and we feel we're living on the edges of life, numbed by onslaughts great and small. But as I am realizing from my own experience, we don't have to be "beaten down." God's mercies are new every day, and they are freely available.

I don't know what your bad year holds for you. One friend who'd had a series of bad years told me, "Forget the *one* bad year! How about my whole life?" We all go through tough times. The point is to see them for what they are, and to respond in a way that allows good to come out of the bad.

I've come to believe that our heavenly Father can bring good out of every bad thing that happens here on earth. Though we live in a broken world where pain and loss and sickness abound, our loving God redeems all the suffering that Satan has unleashed on the world. Believing this, we walk by faith, not by sight, knowing that nothing comes to us except the Father allow it.

Years ago, there was a much-admired elderly woman in our community named Mrs. Cooksey. A friend asked her the secret of her exemplary life. She looked up, a little twinkle in her eyes, and gave this one-word answer: "Trouble!"

I've written this book in two parts: Part 1 is written for you in the first days and weeks of crisis. When a huge wave of pain knocks us down, we can't think about how we're going to reach the shore; all we can do is try to keep our heads above water. Part 1 will give you some emergency tactics to help you stay afloat. Then, in Part 2 I've shared some strategies that will help you through the long haul—that will show you how to navigate the stormy waters of pain and make your way to the peaceful shore.

Yes, your life right now is difficult. It seems impossible. But it is your life, in all its complexity and beauty. Stop and see it for what it is: acknowledge your losses and disappointments, but be mindful of your blessings as well. As we go through this year together, remember that God has promised to be with you and that He will never leave you or forsake you, no matter what.

There is no permanent calamity for any child of God;
Way stations all, at which we briefly stop
Upon our homeward road.

Our pain and grief are only travel stains which shall be wiped away,
Within the blessed warmth and light of home,
By God's own hand some day.
—Author Unknown

PART ONE

Emergency Help
for When the Crisis Hits

Save me, O God! For the waters have come up to my neck.
I sink in deep mire, where there is no standing;
I have come into deep waters, Where the floods overflow me.
I am weary with my crying . . .
My eyes fail while I wait for my God.

—Psalm 69:1-3

If knowing answers to life's questions
is absolutely necessary to you, then forget the journey.
You will never make it,
for this is a journey of unknowables—
of unanswered questions, enigmas, incomprehensibles,
and most of all, things unfair.

—Madame Jeanne Guyon[1]

CHAPTER ONE
"I Can't Do This"

So, THINGS HAPPEN. One minute you're sailing through life on peaceful waters, when all of a sudden, from out of nowhere, a giant wave capsizes your safe existence—and life is never the same again. An unexpected loss can knock all the breath out of you and send you plunging into dark waters, where you are instantly paralyzed. Fear, shock, and confusion flood in, and you are thrust into shutdown mode. We know we have to keep going, but how?

Or perhaps you're experiencing a sense of loss that has developed over time. Gathering clouds hover overhead, and you have a growing awareness that some unnamed dread is approaching—you can feel your joy and purpose hopelessly slipping away. How will you find your way through these murky waters? Or maybe there's a problem or issue in your life that you've tried to ignore and now it's finally erupted. You're forced to stop your life and refocus your attention.

My own bad year grew out of a series of less eventful ones that we managed to cruise through—until one October day four years ago when I realized there was no getting through this one. Not without a lot of tears and pain, at least.

Being a mom was all I wanted. In a span of ten years, my husband, Bill, and I had four wonderful, energetic, fun-loving little boys. My life was perfect. Almost. It just seemed that someone was missing. Though each of our four sons is priceless, I knew how it worked: "A son's a son 'til he takes a wife; a daughter's a daughter all of her life." How would I get my daughter to round out my perfect life? The logical solution was adoption. Simple.

After two or three years of paperwork and a roller-coaster search, Bill and our four sons—Jon, Eric, Chris, and Andy (ages fourteen down to eight)—and I were at the Seattle airport waiting to pick up our daughter, Kim Yung Ja. She was three and a half years old; thirty-six inches tall; had short, dark, straight hair; and had spent most of her life in an orphanage north of Seoul. A volunteer carried her off the plane and placed her in our arms. We were enchanted by our tiny little daughter and renamed her Amy Kim Carmichael. We then proceeded to make her a Carmichael. Or tried to.

You can imagine her transition. She came from a place where everyone looked like her to a place where the people had round eyes, blond hair, and a strange language. And with no say in the matter, she found herself plopped into a family and expected to be like them.

If you had asked me twenty-one years ago to tell you about adoption, I would have spoken of it in glowing terms: the perfect solution for infertile couples or for parents like me with a yearning that just won't go away.

But that was before the most traumatic year of our family's life. What would I tell you now about adoption? Imagine accepting an amputated arm from another person and attaching it to your own body—hoping the graft will take.

When Amy was in her early twenties, she decided she wanted to live on her own. She began to have a lot of fun—far too much fun. We heard rumors of her being involved in out-of-control partying. I wondered, *Who is this person? How can she just "wig out" like that?*

My sons and daughters-in-law warned, "If she doesn't change her ways, there's a train wreck ahead." We spent sleepless nights praying and worrying. We tried to talk sense to her. We tried tough love. We consulted professionals. I knew something strange was going on in her life, but she was twenty-one, so there was only so much we could do.

One October Friday, as I prepared to go out of town for a speaking engagement, I sensed an urgency to connect with Amy, so I asked if she could meet me at Red Robin for lunch. She agreed and showed up looking very depressed. I ordered my usual chicken salad, and she ordered her usual rice bowl. "How are you, Amy?" I asked.

"Not so good. One of my friends at work is pregnant and her boyfriend doesn't want to marry her."

"Oh . . . What is she going to do?"

"Everybody's telling her to get an abortion."

"What do you think?"

"I don't think that would be right."

"Well, what about her family?"

She gave a little sigh of disgust. "Oh, if her family found out, they'd disown her." By this time, my heart was beginning to pound. "Amy, will you tell your friend we'll be glad to help her if she wants help?"

Later in the car, she burst into tears: "Mom, it's me! *I'm* pregnant." Then she said, "Now I know how my birth mother felt. There's no way I can be a mom now. I'm going to place the baby for adoption."

Stunned into momentary silence, I thought, *Maybe she's wrong; maybe she isn't pregnant after all.* And then I said what countless other mothers have said to their daughters: "Honey, we'll get through this." That's what we parents do—we go into automatic overdrive and do what we must to help our family. Rescue the survivors. I suddenly realized I had just joined a vast club of mothers— a club I'd never wanted to join. This was not my dream for my daughter.

> I suddenly realized I had just joined a vast club of mothers—a club I'd never wanted to join.

I took her back to her apartment, and we sat on her bed and cried and prayed together. I told her to hang on, that we'd get through this, and to wait until Monday, when we could go to the doctor. I knew I had to go home and tell Bill, and then somehow go on to my speaking engagement. *Where had I gone wrong, where had I failed her? How could we have avoided this?*

As I drove, waves of anger, shock, and grief poured over me.

How can Amy handle another life-defining loss? How can I walk through this with her? I can't do this!

Although things looked impossible for all of us at the time, later on we would be amazed at how God directed our steps in the confusing and painful months ahead.

You, LORD, are my shepherd. I will never be in need. . . .
You are true to your name, and you lead me along the right paths.
I may walk through valleys as dark as death, but I won't be afraid.
—PSALM 23:1, 3–4 CEV

Stories of Loss

In the following pages, we'll take an up-close look into the lives of several people who were unexpectedly thrashed by overwhelming waves of loss. In these true stories, you just might see reflections of your own experiences or of those you love and care for. The camaraderie we feel in knowing that others have walked this way before us brings much-needed comfort and the hope that you, too, will survive your own bad year.

No test or temptation that comes your way is beyond
the course of what others have had to face.
All you need to remember is that God will never let you down;
he'll never let you be pushed past your limit;
he'll always be there to help you come through it.
—1 CORINTHIANS 10:13, *The Message*

"I'm Bankrupt. I've Lost Everything!"

Brad and his wife, Susan, were small retail owners in their late fifties and had worked hard to get where they were. Retirement was just around the corner, and they looked forward to having weekends free. Their dream was to ride their motorcycles across the country.

When Brad's parents passed away, he and Susan were surprised to realize they had a sizable chunk of money to invest. After investigating several possibilities to get the best possible return on their investment, they decided to buy into a real estate venture in California. The real estate market was booming, and they were assured that this was a "slam dunk." They sold their small business and added that to the investment as well, and then looked forward to a comfortable life.

Who could have foreseen the rapid economic downturn, with the foreclosures and bankruptcies that followed? A lot of people didn't—and certainly not Brad and Susan. One morning when Brad didn't receive his monthly payment from the real estate company, he called the CEO's office and got a recording that said the phone had been disconnected. Worried, he made several other phone calls, only to be told that the company he had invested everything in had just filed for bankruptcy.

Brad felt as if he'd been punched in the stomach. He said, "You read about it every day, but when it happens to you, it's an earthquake." He finally reached an attorney who represented the company and was told, "It may be a good idea for you to get a job."

Numb with shock, he and Susan realized that, almost overnight, they had no income. What could he do, at his age, to provide for his family—to simply pay the bills?

It was humiliating, embarrassing. Fear descended upon him, wrapping him in its clutches, smothering him until he could hardly breathe.

Sure, they had their faith, but how would they get through this

> Fear descended upon him, wrapping him in its clutches, smothering him until he could hardly breathe.

one? Forget a comfortable retirement; how would they survive? At the time, stress was their constant companion; but Brad and Susan were to discover a God who would lead them through an impossible journey to know His provision in ways they could never have imagined.

Surely, goodness and mercy shall follow me
all the days of my life.
Thus says the LORD who makes a way in the sea
and a path through the mighty waters. . . .
Do not remember the former things, nor consider the things of old.
Behold, I will do a new thing.
—ISAIAH 43:16, 18

"I Don't Want to Be Married to You Anymore"

Jim McClelland is a big guy, a gentle guy. He was in his ninth year of being a youth pastor, and he loved every minute of his work. He'd been married to Lindsay for eight years, and they had two young sons, a preschooler and a first-grader. Sure, there were challenges and tensions, but Jim was unaware of the crisis building inside Lindsay.

One August day, Lindsay asked Jim to sit down in the living room so they could talk. What she said rocked his world: "Jim, I don't want to be married anymore."

"*What?* What are you talking about?"

To Jim, there were three cornerstones in his life: Jesus, the Bible, and Lindsay. A three-legged stool. What she was telling him did not compute. What he was hearing knocked the props out from under him.

> "I was absolutely deconstructed. . . . Destroyed."

But she was resolute. Matter-of-fact.

Jim told me, "I was absolutely deconstructed. Do you remember the pile of rubble left by the bombing of the World Trade Center?

Or the explosion of the *Challenger?* That was me. Destroyed. I couldn't even talk about it."

Jim and Lindsay went for counseling, but her mind was made up.

In those dark days, Jim was certain all was lost. He felt utterly alone. Lindsay wanted to stay together through Christmas, so the boys wouldn't have negative emotions connected to the holiday. Somehow they made it through. After Christmas, they went through their belongings, sorting them into piles: "That's mine; that's yours."

Jim said, "It was so weird, standing in the garage with all my stuff, my dreams in cardboard boxes. But then—I don't know how he knew—my friend, my best man, showed up in my driveway, got out, and just started in, helping me pack.

"We didn't say three words. There was no conversation. But he was *there*. For seven months after that, the boys and I lived with my friend and his family. The boys and I didn't have beds—just sleeping bags on the floor. The boys didn't care so much—they thought they were camping—but one night I stood and looked at them sleeping on the floor in this tiny one-bedroom apartment, and I cried. It was the lowest of the low times. I went from a guy who never cried to one who cried all the time."

How would he get through, rebuild? Would he ever be the same, ever be happy again? And what about his ministry? What would his church think? Although life would never be the same for Jim, he was to discover a God who never let him go.

> *I, the* LORD *have called You in righteousness,*
> *and will hold Your hand; I will keep You."*
> —ISAIAH 42:6A

"They Can't Find Your Mother"

Julie Wilson's mom, Deede, was a vibrant, fifty-four-year-old real estate agent living in Southern California. She had recently gotten out of a destructive marriage, and life finally seemed good again. Julie was blond and vivacious like her mother, Deede, and was on her way to a much-anticipated girlfriends trip to Cabo San Lucas, Mexico. Julie and Deede had planned to meet at Los Angeles International Airport during Julie's layover, so they could catch up over coffee. But Julie's mother never showed. When her mother didn't call, Julie assumed her cellphone battery had died and that she'd been delayed in traffic. Julie continued on her journey.

Julie said, "My two friends and I got to our beautiful resort in Cabo, but somehow the whole day was strange. Something wasn't right. On the surface, everything seemed perfect—we started the day with hot-stone massages and spent time at the pool. Then we went into the town of Cabo San Lucas. But shortly after we left the resort, I felt the urgent need to get back. I tried to shake it off and enjoy the day, assuring myself that everything was okay. Our first stop was at an Internet café so we could check e-mail. I was surprised not to have heard from my mother, so I e-mailed her, telling her how much fun I was having with my girlfriends. I knew she would be so happy for me."

Julie and her friends finished checking their e-mail, then briefly walked down some side streets, shopping. But Julie couldn't shake a strong sense of concern that something was wrong and suggested they go back to the resort. At the resort, they had a delicious dinner on the beach, but still, she felt uneasy.

Julie said, "We left and went up to our room, and I found a message from my husband, Pete, on the phone. I panicked, as my first thought was that something had happened to Gracie—my one-year-old daughter, whom I'd left for the first time. My best friend, Vivian, was with me as I called him back.

Pete's first words were, "Is Vivian there with you?"

"Yes. What's going on?"

"I just got off the phone with your brother, Michael. Julie, they can't find your mother."

Julie ran to the bathroom and threw up. She said, "I knew immediately that Mom was not alive. And I knew that Erwin, my stepfather, had killed her."

> "I knew immediately that Mom was not alive."

They soon heard that Deede's body had been discovered, murdered. Her stepfather was ultimately charged. Julie would eventually be called to testify at the trial.

How does a daughter get through a living nightmare such as this? And where was God in all of this? For Julie, this traumatic event colored every waking moment of the days to come. But later, when she attended her mother's trial, she felt the grace of God surrounding her and keeping her.

When you pass through the waters,
I will be with you; and through the rivers
they shall not overflow you.
When you walk through the fire, you shall not be burned.
—ISAIAH 43:2

"Depression . . . Something I Know"

Jason Clark was a brilliant pastor of a leading church in the UK, the father of three, and a university professor. He has done a lot in his life, and he was just this side of forty.

When Jason was nearly seventeen, he became a Christian at a wonderful church. He says, "I remember the first experience of being prayed for—having people lay hands on me, gently, lovingly; and it was the beginning of healing in my life. Church was wonderful: a place full of brothers, sisters, aunts and uncles, adopted mums and dads; a place where I was loved and cared for."

For the first time in his life, people built him up and spoke words of life into who he was and what he could be. His home life had been very different. As a child, he had to be the adult. He remembers running out in the snow in his pajamas, barefoot, chasing his mother down the street, begging her not to take the overdose she'd threatened to take. He remembers hiding in the closet for hours as he heard his parents destroy each other and their house. Then there was the pain of missing college to care for his one-year-old brother, pretending to be his father whenever they went out in public.

These things were regular occurrences in his life, and in the midst of destruction, he determined not to be like his parents.

After he became a Christian, things went well for a while. He grew and moved on. He went to seminary and college and married. Yet he found himself coping less and less as anxiety and depression began to hit him harder and harder. Only in hindsight did he understand that he'd suffered from depression as a child. He'd had a brief respite for two or three years, when he initially became a Christian, but old pains began to resurface as life moved on.

In spite of growing anxiety, Jason pressed on. He worked a hundred hours a week to support his family, commuted three hours a day, and raised a young family, all the while planting the church he hoped to someday pastor full-time. His mounting depression and anxiety were kept at bay only by working harder and harder. His first day of being a full-time pastor finally arrived. He celebrated this momentous day by having a nervous breakdown. Throughout the day, he rotated between being catatonic and suffering panic attacks. He thought he was dying, or going insane. His body, brain, soul, and mind finally gave in to an inevitable collapse.

He says, "It was tough on my wife. All I could do was get up, see the kids off to school, go back to bed, get up when the kids came home, and preach on Sunday. How I did that, I have no idea. Our church was wonderful. They told me that I had always said it was okay to be ill, and now it was my turn. During this time the church grew."

Jason got medication and went into therapy, and he began to face up to his past and the abuse he'd never dealt with before. The coping mechanism he'd developed—caring for others to make up for his own lack of care—had found an unhealthy place in the church. It was easy to excel in church by caring. As a nineteen-year-old, he had led small groups and ministries with adults. He'd seen his leadership role as having an "old head on young shoulders."

He was determined not to be his parents, to not do what they did or be who they were. This determination had helped him survive, but it finally came undone one day in therapy when his therapist asked, "Why do you define your life by who you *don't* want to be, rather than who you *do?*" Jason realized in that moment that he had spent so many years as a workaholic, pushing, striving, and fearful that he would become his parents.

"Why do you define your life by who you *don't* want to be, rather who you *do?*"

At the lowest point of his breakdown, Jason felt as if he were losing his faith. The questions and doubts he'd kept at bay came crashing in, demanding to be faced. One night, Jason took his Bible to bed and held it to his chest; he told God he didn't know how to read it anymore, and this was as close as he could get to it. He hoped it was okay with God.

Jason says, "Now I know it was, and is. During that devastating time, I realized that Jesus was still the same Jesus I had given my life to. It was the systems I'd built up that had fallen apart. So I went back to seminary to do part-time research in theology and to think through the things I was realizing. Theology saved my faith. And theology created something new in my life, and in our church. As it helped me grow, it helped our church grow.

"I know I have a long way to go and may suffer many dark days until I die. Genetics and a family disposition to depression mean I will often wrestle with life. But in the wrestling, I find dependence on Christ, and I find re-creation and new life.

"The pattern of destruction and fear I knew as a child has abated. It has not been passed on to my wife, my children. In them and in my church community, I see hope. With them, I do life in the deepest and most painful and joyful and happy ways. My anxiety and depression, like Winston Churchill's 'Black Dog,' is something I know and take for a walk through life."

> *Yes, though I walk through the (deep, sunless)*
> *valley of the shadow of death,*
> *I will fear or dread no evil; for You are with me;*
> *Your rod (to protect) and Your staff (to guide), they comfort me. . . .*
> *You anoint my head with oil; my (brimming) cup runs over.*
> *Surely or only goodness, mercy and unfailing love*
> *shall follow me all the days of my life;*
> *and through the length of days the house of the Lord*
> *(and His presence) shall be my dwelling place.*
> —Psalm 23:4–6 AMP

"A Dreaded Diagnosis"

Jo Franz—an outgoing young wife, mother, and talented singer involved with helping her husband in ministry—had a lot going for her.

One morning she stood in the kitchen, cooking pancakes on the cast-iron griddle for the youth choir, when she suddenly felt as if she were falling over with dizziness. Jo landed in a chair as her husband and the rest of the choir entered the room. Alarmed, she knew she had to deal with a growing set of troubling issues. That year she'd had some strange symptoms, not noticeable to anyone but her. Now she knew there was something seriously wrong with her.

After many tests, the doctor gave her the dreaded diagnosis: multiple sclerosis, a crippling disease. She had suspected the diagnosis, because the symptoms were the same as her friend's, who had MS. Ironically, she had even done fund-raisers for MS research.

It was only later, when she was alone, that she broke down and cried with fear about the unpredictable life MS would bring. But MS was only the beginning of her difficult time. Soon after her diagnosis, she went through an unwanted divorce.

How could Jo live a full, vibrant life with the threat of a disabling disease hanging over her head? In those early, dark days, Jo could never have imagined how God would use her weakness to demonstrate His strength and joy.

> *Those who wait on the* LORD *shall renew* their *strength;*
> *They shall mount up with wings like eagles;*
> *They shall run and not be weary,*
> *They shall walk and not faint.*
> —ISAIAH 40:31

"My World Changed with a Phone Call"

It was a late May afternoon. It had been cleaning day, so there was a sense of fresh order in the house. Karen's husband would be attending a monthly board dinner meeting; her youngest daughter, Sommer, was away for the evening. Karen looked forward to throwing a simple salad together for her solo supper.

Karen took a deep breath and savored the quiet in her home. She smiled, thinking of Sommer's upcoming high school graduation and acceptance into college. Soon Karen and Bob would be empty-nesters—it was here already. Their oldest daughter, Hillary, had recently married a wonderful young man, and the newlyweds had moved to the Midwest to finish their education.

It was a new era for her and Bob. They had treasured every minute of parenting, but now it was time to let go.

The phone rang, interrupting Karen's solitude. It was Hillary. But something was not right. Karen listened with growing alarm, as Hillary's speech seemed strange. There was something very wrong. Numb with shock and suppressed fear, she responded with supernatural calm, as she said what had to be "words from God."

> Numb with shock and suppressed fear, she responded with supernatural calm.

Karen said, "I finally got my son-in-law,

Kevin, on the phone, and he confirmed that Hillary had been man-ifesting some strange behaviors. She'd been pacing the floors in constant motion, all the while plugged into a music headset. She had quit attending class—highly unusual for her—and was becom-ing reclusive. She also seemed to be having hallucinations and delu-sions.

What could be happening? Karen had no idea what they were facing, and immediately tried to reach her husband, who was in a board meeting, but his phone was on silent. Later he told Karen she'd left him five messages, but she barely had any memory of that. She only knew she had to get to her daughter.

Kevin agreed that Karen should come immediately, and Karen got online to check flights and availability, briefly aghast at the last-minute prices; however, nothing mattered but getting there.

Over the next few months, Karen and her family began to dis-cover that Hillary had had a psychotic break, and it appeared that she had schizoaffective disorder. One psychiatrist told them there was "less than a 10 percent chance she'll get better in her life-time."

Karen wondered, *How do I parent her in this new place and sup-port my new son-in-law? How is it possible that my dreams and hopes for my child have been so drastically altered? How will we get through this?* Yet Karen and her family were to learn what it means to trust God in a strange new world.

> *He gives power to the weak,*
> *And to* those who have *no might He increases strength.*
> —Isaiah 40:29

"Why Hasn't God Healed Our Little Boy?"

Doug and Angela Tucker were in their second year of planting a church in Athens, Georgia. They loved their people, the chal-lenges of starting a new work, and especially their two children—seven-year-old Aleisha and fifteen-month-old David. In the late spring of 1998, Angela was back at her pre-pregnancy weight, feeling good.

Angela says, "Life seemed to be clicking right along with everything under control. One morning I was outside with some ladies of our church beside the pool. I felt nauseated and thought perhaps I had the flu. One of the women suggested I may be pregnant, but that seemed completely absurd. However, she offered me a pregnancy test that she had left over, as she was currently six weeks pregnant. Much to my surprise, the test was positive. I went home and announced the news to my husband, who was as surprised as I was. But, after adjusting to the news, we were very much looking forward to the birth of this little addition to the Tucker family."

Four months into the pregnancy, Angela went alone to have a sonogram, a routine procedure. The sonographer began her work, and the longer she looked, the more questions she began to ask. Angela had been through this type of questioning before, when she'd had a miscarriage before David. With growing alarm, Angela asked, "What's wrong?"

The sonographer confirmed that the baby was a boy, and then went on to tell Angela that although she wasn't supposed to discuss these things with her, she saw cysts on the baby's brain and a two-vessel umbilical cord instead of three vessels. She told her to come to a neonatologist the next day and have an amniocentesis performed.

Angela was devastated. What did this mean? As she shared the news with Doug, it suddenly seemed very important that the baby had a name. Doug anointed Angela with oil, and they prayed for healing, asking God to give them a name for His child.

Angela says, "Immediately the name Samuel came to my mind, but I didn't voice this to Doug. Later, Doug asked me to research the name Samuel on the computer to see what it meant. We found that Samuel meant 'heard of God.' We believed that God would hear our prayer and heal our child."

Nothing was discovered from the amniocentesis except what Samuel didn't have. He didn't have Down syndrome, and he didn't have myriad other chromosome problems. With each visit to the neonatologist, new problems were discovered: a hole in Samuel's heart, possibly webbed fingers and toes. They were told that *if* Samuel made it through the trauma of birth, he would very likely die within a few hours. Two doctors told Angela that she needed to abort Samuel.

> They were told that *if* Samuel made it through the trauma of birth, he would very likely die within a few hours.

Angela said, "My heart sank beneath the depths of despair. This was the worst news I had ever had to endure in my entire life. My husband and I gathered our faith and the support of our church members and family and went through week after week of this very unstable pregnancy with Samuel. We prayed, believing that God would heal this child and that when he came from the womb, he would be as normal as any child ever born. This was not to be God's answer."

After a difficult delivery, Samuel finally arrived around five o'clock on January 23, 1999. He did not have a hole in his heart nor did he have webbed fingers and toes. He did, however, have very short arms and legs in proportion to the rest of his body, and he could not get enough oxygen in.

Within hours, Samuel was transferred to a children's hospital by ambulance. Angela said, "Everything happened so fast. We were asked to sign papers saying that if Samuel died on the way, we would not hold the hospital responsible. We were told that we could not follow the ambulance for safety reasons, so they allowed us to leave before the ambulance. On the three-hour trip to Augusta, the ambulance passed us with flashing lights. The most horrifying feeling came over us, as we knew that our precious little boy was inside, fighting for his life."

Anxious days passed, filled with tests and consultations before it was discovered that Samuel had rhizomelic chondrodysplasia punctata, or RCDP, a genetic bone disorder. Samuel's cells were missing an enzyme that allowed the body to grow. Doug and Angela discovered they were both carriers of the gene and that both parents had to drop the gene down at the same time for a child to be affected. They learned that Aleisha and David were very likely carriers, but because they didn't receive the gene from both of their parents, they did not have the syndrome.

The prognosis wasn't good. One day in a consultation, Doug and Angela were told that Samuel would more than likely not live to be twelve weeks old—a year at the most. They were also told that Samuel was severely retarded. Angela waited until the doctor left the room, and then fell on the floor, begging God to heal her child.

An exhausting saga ensued—tubes, treatments, procedures, and learning how to care for Samuel at home. The early months of Samuel's life were a confusing time for Angela, a time of questioning. She agonized, *Why hasn't God healed our little boy? After all, we've believed His Word, we've lived a holy standard of life, and we're serving God with all we have in us. How can I trust Him to save me if I can't trust him to heal Samuel?*

Angela and Doug had no idea then how Samuel would change their lives. How much they would learn, or how their ministry would change in deep and meaningful ways.

> *He will feed his flock like a shepherd.*
> *He will gather the lambs with His arm,*
> *and carry* them *in His bosom,*
> And *gently lead those who are with young.*
> —Isaiah 40:11

To You, in the Midst of Crisis

The stories and pains we've shared thus far in this chapter are not unusual. All of us—if we live long enough—travel unwanted paths where we face seemingly insurmountable enemies. But even though pain and loss are common to us all, when it enters our own life, it can shake us to the core; and we are desperate for help. God has provided just the help we need.

Know That the Battle Is Not Yours

There's a story in the Bible about a time when the Israelites faced overwhelming odds as enormous armies were coming from all around to attack them, to wipe them out. They were completely outnumbered.

Their leader, Jehosaphat, didn't know what to do. But he called the people to fast and pray. They desperately needed to hear from God to know what to do in this overwhelming situation. After fasting and praying, the people received a word from God: "This is what the LORD says to you: 'Do not be afraid or discouraged because of this vast army. For the battle is not yours, but God's. . . . You will not have to fight this battle. Take up your positions; stand firm and see the deliverance the LORD will give you, O Judah and Jerusalem. Do not be afraid; do not be discouraged. Go out to face them tomorrow, and the LORD will be with you.'" (2 Chronicles 20:15, 17).

Remember That Your Crisis Is Just for a Season

In our family's crisis, there were principles from God's Word that spoke to us deeply. For weeks I prayed Psalm 23 on my daily walks: "Though I walk through the valley of the shadow . . ." *Through!* In all my years of reading the twenty-third Psalm, I'd never seen the word *through* before with such vivid understanding. The word *through* gave me hope; it said that our family wouldn't *stay* in the valley. Yes, we were in a valley, but it was only for a season.

> Yes, we were in a valley, but it was only for a season.

The crisis you are in at the moment isn't forever. You won't make a permanent *home* in the valley, and even while you are there, you are not alone.

Trust God, Even When No Answers Are in Sight

The question is not so much what to do, but whom to turn to. As Angela said, "We learned to run to Him and not from Him."

In our family's situation, we did not see a good endgame. How could we help our daughter place the only flesh and blood she knew in the arms of another family? How could we do such a thing? We love our babies. How do you love and let go? *Impossible.*

> How could we help our daughter place the only flesh and blood she knew in the arms of another family?

There appeared to be no pain-free solution. Neither Amy nor the birth father felt ready for marriage or parenthood. We were concerned that the child could be bounced back and forth if she stayed in our family. How would we solve this? We studied all the angles, over and over.

This is where you're hoping I tell you that if you do *A* and *B*, you will get *C*. How I wish I could, but sometimes life is not like that. In John, chapter 9, the Pharisees brought the blind man to Jesus and asked Him, "Who sinned, this man or his parents, that he was born blind?" They wanted answers. *Reasons.* Whose fault is this?

We often romanticize how things should be, maybe from our propensity to want a story with a happy ending. But some things defy easy answers and formulas. Sometimes we live with a mess for a while.

Jesus answered, "Neither this man nor his parents sinned . . . but this happened so that the work of God might be displayed in his life" (John 9:3–7 NIV), and then Jesus went on to heal the man. There can be a higher purpose, a deeper meaning in life's twists and turns. We don't have to know all the answers when we stand in the truth that the battle is not ours, but God's. Letting go in the midst of a crisis is completely opposite of what we want to do, but doing so is our only true hope for victory.

Know That You Are Not Alone

Sure, you feel alone. Feeling alone seems to be a common thread when you hit that "lowest of the low" place. You are left with a sense of helplessness and impotence, and fear can choke you. Songwriter Bobby Bare said in the song "Lonesome Valley," "You gotta walk that lonesome valley . . . all by yourself." But, the reality is that even though no other person walks with us, we are *not* alone. The psalmist said, "Though I walk through the valley of the shadow . . . I will not fear, for *You are with me.*"

Jacob, running away from home, slept on a rock under the stars. *Alone!* But he was awestruck by the presence of God: "Surely the Lord is in this place, and I did not know *it* . . . How awesome *is* this place!" (Genesis 28:16, 17). The abiding presence of the Lord dissipated his fear, his loneliness.

Years later, Jacob returned to face his brother, Esau, whom he'd cheated out of an inheritance. The night before he encountered Esau, Jacob wrestled alone with the angel on the distant side of the river: "Then Jacob was left alone; and the Man wrestled with him until the breaking of the day" (Genesis 32:24).

There is something purifying about being alone. It's where you're confronted with what you're really all about—where your strength lies, what your rock-bottom motivations are. Gail Sheehy, in writing about the passages of life, said: "The older we grow, the more we become aware of the commonality of our lives, as well as our essential aloneness as navigators through the human journey."[2]

But you are not truly alone, even if you feel like it. Again, the psalmist said, "Where can I go from Your Spirit? Or where can I flee from Your presence? If I ascend into heaven, You are there. If I make my bed in hell, behold, You are there. If I take the wings of the morning, and dwell in the uttermost parts of the sea, even there Your hand shall lead me, and Your right hand shall hold me. The darkness and the light are both alike to You" (Psalm 139:7–10, 12).

Hold On

It's important to remember that, in the initial stage of crisis, we're not always thinking clearly. We don't have all the facts yet, and fear and grief can smother hope. Try not to panic. It may not be as bad as you think. It may be worse than you think. The main thing is to wait on God and hold on tight.

When we're in pain, we're tempted to run away, escape, distract ourselves with mind-numbing activities. It is only human. Even Jesus Himself looked to the cross with dread. He prayed in the garden: "My Father! If it is possible, let this cup of suffering be taken away from me!" Then he added, "Yet I want your will, not mine." And so we, too, are held by love, caught by commitment, ensnared by our relationships.

> We, too, are held by love, caught by commitment, ensnared by our relationships.

One night I wrote in my prayer journal: "Lord, I feel so exposed. . . . I want to stay home, to avoid places and people that should feel safe, but don't." And yet, we go on, even though we don't know how. We keep living, even if we don't feel like it. We muddle through an impossible place, even though there's no fine print on how to do it.

> *Do not fear, for I am with you; do not be dismayed,*
> *for I am your God. I will strengthen you and help you;*
> *I will uphold you with my righteous right hand."*
> —ISAIAH 41:10

God holds for you new dreams and fresh possibilities. He is indeed near to your breaking heart, and it is indeed true that through His mercies we are not consumed (Lamentations 3:22). In the midst of despair, there is hope. Things can get better. The sun will come up in the morning.

Hold on, my friend. Don't look at what is going on around you; hold on to what you know—*God is.* And no matter how it looks, know that God can make a way when there seems to be no way.

> *When I am walking in darkness, on shifting ground,*
> *remind me that you are still leading me by the hand . . .*
> *no matter that I cannot feel your touch.*
> *Remind me when I am passing through even the driest place*
> *that you are ahead of me,*
> *opening secret springs of water for my soul. Amen.*
> —YOU SET MY SPIRIT FREE; JOHN OF THE CROSS[3]

PERSONAL REFLECTION

Read Psalm 23 meditatively, slowly. If possible, read it in different versions over several days, choosing a different version of Psalm 23 for each day. Take time to reflect on each verse; praying as you read.

1. In your prayer journal, rewrite Psalm 23, personalizing it: (e.g., "You, Lord, are my shepherd. I can relax into Your care, knowing You care for my every need," etc.).

2. Ask yourself, "At this place in my life, how is He comforting me? Restoring me?"

3. What does it mean for me to "lie down beside still waters"?

4. Do any words or phrases in Psalm 23 speak to you more than others? Write them down and expand on them.

Scripture to Give You Courage

Let us hold fast the confession of our hope without wavering, for He who promised is faithful (Hebrews 10:23 NASB).

Come to Me, all you that labor and are heavy laden, and I will give you rest (Matthew 11:28 KJV).

As a father pities his children, so the LORD pities those who fear Him. For He knows our frame; He remembers that we are dust (Psalm 103:13, 14 NKJV).

Wait on the Lord; Be of good courage, and He shall strengthen your heart; Wait, I say, on the LORD (Psalm 27:14 NKJV)!

Be strong and of good courage, do not fear nor be afraid of them; for the LORD your God, He is the One who goes with you. He will not leave you nor forsake you (Deuteronomy 31:6 NKJV).

Have I not commanded you? Be strong and of good courage; do not be afraid, nor be dismayed, for the LORD your God is with you wherever you go (Joshua 1:9 NKJV).

But Jesus immediately said to them: "Take courage! It is I. Don't be afraid" (Matthew 14:27 NIV).

These things I have spoken to you, so that in Me you may have peace. In the world you have tribulation, but take courage; I have overcome the world (John 16:33 NASB).

Who still thinks there is some device
(if only he could find it)
which will make pain not to be pain?
It doesn't really matter whether you grip the arms
of the dentist's chair or let your hands lie in your lap.
The drill drills on.

—C. S. Lewis[1]

CHAPTER TWO

It Hurts to Lose

A FTER SURGERY, THE doctor asked his patient, "On a scale of one to ten, what would you say is your pain level?"

How do you measure pain? While pain is universal, it is also individual. Pain comes in different degrees, and it's just part of being alive. So is loss. I just lost a favorite necklace. Big deal, but it bothers me. My eleven-year-old nephew lost one of his shoes on a camping trip. ("How did you manage to lose one shoe?" his mother asked.) Just this week, Bill and I lost a chunk of our retirement money in the stock market fall. A much bigger deal—a loss we've yet to come to terms with.

Different Losses, Different Pain

As long as we're alive, we suffer loss and pain in varying degrees. Some losses radically alter the contours of our lives—and we wake up to realize that life as we know it has taken an unwelcome turn. Other losses are ragged, leaving unfinished business and jagged edges. And then there are those losses that are perhaps the most frightening of all: those irrevocable losses that come through the jaws of death.

Life-altering Loss

A life-altering loss can be a life-defining illness, such as Jo Franz being diagnosed with multiple sclerosis or Angela and Doug's baby being born with so many disabilities. Such losses force us to come to terms with the reality of what we actually have compared to what we dreamed we'd have.

Jim McClelland had a life-altering loss when his wife told him that it was over between them—no matter their joint investment in their two little boys and their ministry. His life-altering loss went on to become a ragged loss as he adjusted to the reality of shared custody of his two sons. Some losses don't fall into a "neat" category—they overlap, pile on, and compound.

Losing all of your life's savings just as you are about to retire can certainly change life, as Brad and Susan discovered. It altered their image of themselves as the grandparents who could take their grandchildren to Disneyland at the drop of a hat or the ones who always picked up the tab in the restaurant for family dinners out. That ended, as they scrambled to survive amid the wreck of their dreams for retirement.

Loss can show itself as a slow awareness that life will never be the same, as Karen began to realize when her beautiful, talented daughter, Hillary, was diagnosed with schizoaffective disorder. She had to learn how to parent her daughter in new ways and how to support her son-in-law as he loved and cared for Hillary.

My friend Sharlie's loss was more complicated. She cared for her father, who suffered from dementia. She had promised him she would never put him in one of "those places." But as his Alzheimer's progressed, the inevitable became clear. For her own sake and that of her husband and children, she knew he needed help beyond what she could give. The day she drove away from the memory-care facility where she placed her father was one of the darkest days of her life. She drove straight to a bookstore and began looking through books, turning page after page in search of someone who would "not tell me what to *do*, but how to *live through* the darkness." She desperately needed hope to get through it, to know it wasn't her fault and that she had done the best she could.

> *Though I walk in the midst of trouble, You will revive me. . . .*
> *The* LORD *will perfect* *that which* *concerns*
> *Me; Your mercy, O* LORD, *endures* *forever.*
> —PSALM 138:7–8

Ragged Loss

A ragged loss isn't always easy to define. For instance, it's when your children leave home for the first time. You still have children, but they're not there. Or maybe it is having a parent who has forgotten your name. She still has the face of your mother—her voice, her smile—but now, you are the parent. Or perhaps it's moving to a new place, and you miss home. Or the lost feeling you have after you've left a job that was a big part of your identity. Perhaps it is the rupture of an important relationship, and while life is supposed to be going on by now, your heart is still torn.

Joan Chittister, in her book *Scarred by Struggle*, said, "Everybody in the world—including you and me—has stories of pain and grief, depression and despair, hopelessness and sorrow. Some of them we survived well. Some of them we didn't. . . . There is no such thing as life without struggle."[2]

My own family's loss in the relinquishment of our granddaughter had a beginning, a middle, and a culmination. But, as in divorce, our loss is a *ragged loss*, as we grapple day by day with the unfolding implications of an open adoption. From the beginning, Amy wanted an open adoption—she wanted to know her child, and she wanted her child to know her. Amy did not waver from this.

How does open adoption work? I felt as if I were out to sea with no compass or bearings. What will happen after, to Amy, to the baby?

We are fortunate that the family who eventually adopted Anna-belle has opened their arms to us generously and graciously, in un-believable ways. More than words can say, we are grateful. I know that most adoption situations are not like ours. But our loss contin-ues to be a ragged one.

As we researched to find just the right family, Amy and Jeff, the birth father, came out for a weekend to go over résumés of poten-tial families. They pored over them, eliminating some, keeping some. As we talked to prospective parents, I remembered what it was like to do the home study when we adopted Amy—you put your heart and soul out there for others to investigate and prod. It takes a lot of guts to adopt, and I felt motherly toward them, too. We had several evenings of "meet the prospective parents."

One day Amy told me, "I call the baby Yung Ja." That's Amy's Korean name, and it means "Little One." Amy showed me with her hands how long her baby was and the size of her tiny feet.

One night in a seafood restaurant in a corner booth, we sat with a prospective couple, Dirk and Joan Zeller. The journey that had brought us to this moment in Amy's seventh month of preg-nancy had been an emotional roller coaster. The couple Amy and Jeff had originally chosen had just been told by their adoption agency that they were not qualified to proceed with the adoption as it was too close to their first adoption.

Dirk and Joan had been praying for God's leading to adopt an-other child, as they already had a four-year-old son. Sitting with them at dinner felt comfortable, natural. Everyone seemed to think, *This is it.* Joan said, "Amy, tell us your heart for your baby."

Amy began to talk of what it was like to be abandoned by her birth mother and how important it was that her baby not feel aban-doned or rejected. Amy said, "For most of my life, I've pretty much thought about myself, but now it's not all about me. It's about my child, and I want her to know I love her enough to give her the best." My husband and I were in awe at the eloquence and strength in our daughter's face and in her words. Shortly after, Amy and Jeff chose Dirk and Joan.

Then, on a warm June day after a long, complicated labor and delivery, we welcomed Annabelle Joy into the world—eight pounds, four ounces of pink and white, with dark curly hair. Exquisite! Now we knew what Amy looked like as a baby. Our sons, our daughters-in-law, and their children came to be with us; and Jeff was with Amy every step of the way. Amy kept Annabelle in her room, and for two days, we laughed, cried, and held her. We took pictures with aunts and uncles and little cousins.

The Zellers were there, too, hearts open and ready. They were thrilled—and we were, too—yet saying hello for them meant saying good-bye for us. On Monday the Zellers brought their legal papers and a notary to witness Amy's signature. A social worker talked to Jeff and Amy privately to make sure they were ready to do this. Yes, they both said. So at three thirty in the afternoon, in the presence of the adoptive parents, my husband read the legal papers to Amy. She sobbed deeply, but signed. I left the hospital that day thinking, *Our family will never be the same.*

> I left the hospital that day thinking, *Our family will never be the same.*

Tuesday was going-home day. Some of our family and close friends arrived. Dirk and Joan came with some of their family. A combination of joy and sorrow, dread and anticipation filled the room. Our pastor offered a mercifully short prayer. Bill placed the baby in Amy's arms, and Amy slowly shuffled across the room, sobbing. I walked beside her. Dirk and Joan put their arms around her and Annabelle in a three-way hug.

A moment of great joy and sorrow. A sacred, terrible moment. Our hearts bled.

Dirk and Joan left with Annabelle, and we took our daughter home.

The world should have stopped going around, but it didn't. Sunrise, coffee, morning routines continued. What is there to say? Having adopted my daughter, I knew the joy of adoption, as well as the challenges. Now I know the other side of it: the side of loss. This ragged loss is one we are still experiencing—and we always will.

Later, Joan wrote me an e-mail:

My Dear Nancie,
My tears today were tears of pain for you and for Amy. God is
allowing my joy to be postponed, so I can grieve for and with you.
I can't even imagine what you must be feeling, I only know that I
hurt because you hurt. "Blessed are those who mourn, for they
shall be comforted." Oh, how I wish I knew the words to bring you
comfort. . . . I will just pray that God will hold you in His arms of
love.
      You and Amy are on my heart.
                              Love, and constant prayers for you,
                                                          Joan

I answered:

Thanks, Joan,
I was thinking it was hard for you to see our grief. And yet we
see your joy, too, which is a great comfort. I think they will both
be part of the bonding and prayer that we now share through
this incredibly beautiful little girl!
      Amy told me that in the middle of her last night with
Annabelle, she snuggled her and thought, "I just can't do this."
But then, the Lord spoke to her and said, "Amy, I have a
wonderful plan for you, for Jeff, and for Annabelle. It's right
that you go ahead with this." Then she told me, "Mom, God
talks to us in our hardest times." She said she felt God's
peace.

I take great comfort in knowing that God values our dreams:

God does not want us to abandon those dreams . . .
but will lovingly work with us
to refine our unrealistic dreams
to restore our broken dreams

to realize our delayed dreams, and
to redesign our shattered dreams
so that both His purposes and our dreams can be fulfilled.
—DAVID SEAMANDS[3]

My brethren, count it all joy when you fall into various trials,
knowing that the testing of your faith produces patience.
But let patience have its perfect work,
that you may be perfect and complete, lacking nothing.
If any of you lacks wisdom, let him ask of God,
who gives to all liberally and without reproach,
and it will be given to him.
—JAMES 1:2–5

Irrevocable Loss

When someone we loves dies, the loss is painfully tangible and irrevocably permanent. C. S. Lewis gives poignant voice to the reality of irrevocable loss when he says,

It is hard to have patience with people who say, "There is no death," or "Death doesn't matter." There is death. And whatever is matters. And whatever happens has consequences, and it and they are irrevocable and irreversible. You might as well say that birth doesn't matter. I look up at the night sky. Is anything more certain than that in all those vast times and spaces, if I were allowed to search them, I should nowhere find her face, her voice, her touch? She died. She is dead. Is the word so difficult to learn?[4]

Some losses are impossible to measure. Job, whose story is told in the Old Testament, lost everything, including all ten of his children. He sighed, "Oh, that my grief were fully weighed" (Job 6:2). How dare I write of my loss in the same chapter as a

parent who stands at the grave of his or her child? I think of my
friend, Sherry Tucker, who lost her eight-year-son, Zach, to brain
cancer. After Zachary showed some troubling symptoms, he went
through medical tests to see what was wrong. It was a devastating
moment for Sherry and Dirk Tucker to learn that their son was
terminally ill with brain cancer.

Sherry writes, "We were being backed into a corner with
nowhere to turn but to our Creator. God was the only light still
shining with hope for Zach."[5] As they began agonizing treatments
to hold the ravenous cancer cells at bay, nothing seemed to work.
Still, Dirk and Sherry and their eleven-year-old daughter, Lexi,
were not ready to face a life without him. Ten months from Zach's
diagnosis of glioblastoma multiforme, Zach left this earth for
heaven. Sherry says, "We will never fully understand why the suffering and devastation occurs to those precious to our hearts . . . [yet]
He does promise to walk with us even in the darkest of moments."[6]

Julie Wilson's irrevocable loss was compounded by the ugly vi-
olence of her mother's murder. A loss such as this brings disbelief,
along with overwhelming emotions of shock and grief and rage and
fear.

The loss of my mother was a big loss for me. She was more like
a close friend, and each of her seven children will insist he or she
was her "favorite." She had that way about her, making each of her
children feel loved. But she did the unthinkable: on a warm, sweet
June morning, she died after a lingering illness.

Everything seemed strange, surreal: phone calls to relay the bad
news, decisions about the funeral, not being able to get my husband on the phone (he was somewhere in Alaska on a speaking engagement). I longed suddenly to be home, to be with my children.
Hug the dogs. Sweep the kitchen floor. Sleep in my own bed. *Call
Mother and tell her what I was going through* . . . I caught myself, reminded of what this was. It was her death—and it was final. I felt
the hollow ache of not having Mother to call. She wasn't there to
say it's going to be all right.

Death, the final enemy, rips loved ones from our lives and can leave us wondering, *Why do we have to lose people we love?*

> *Loved one and friend You have put far from me,*
> And *my acquaintances into darkness.*
> —PSALM 88:18

First Steps in a Crisis

What do you do when life hands you the worst? How do you survive those first few days when your brain is only mush? When the crisis first breaks upon you and you are drowning under the force of the storm, your only job is to keep your head above water—no heroic efforts required. No matter the loss—ragged, life-altering loss, or irrevocable loss—you need to know what step is next. The following three life-giving "tasks" will help you keep afloat in your sea of loss.

Allow God to Hold You—Now

In Mark, chapter 10, we see a tender scene of children coming to Jesus, clambering all over Him. Children instinctively seem to know who is "safe." I love the idea that Jesus was touchable and approachable to children. The disciples tried to chase the children away, but Jesus took the children in His arms and blessed them.

He urges us to come to Him, to come as children—wholehearted, honest, just as we are. We come to Him with our tears, our rage, our grief, our most bitter disappointment. And we come to Him with our questions. Held safe in our Father's embrace, we can ask God the same question Job asked: *Why?* "What is man, that You should . . . test him every moment? How long? Will You not look away from me, and let me alone till I swallow my saliva? Have I sinned? What have I done to You, O watcher of men? Why have You set me as Your target, so that I am a burden to myself?" (Job 7:17–20 NLT).

But while we join Job in his questions, we must also join him in his reverent faith. When Job had lost everything, his wife told him, "Curse God and die!" (Job 2:9 NLT). Just get it over with, Job. End your miserable existence.

While Job didn't mind cursing the day he was born, he wouldn't curse God. He was angry; he was perplexed. Yet in the midst of his misery, he made a breathtaking declaration of faith: "But as for me, I know that my Redeemer lives, and that he will stand upon the earth at last. And after my body was decayed, yet in my body I will see God! I will see him for myself. Yes, I will see him with my own eyes. I am overwhelmed at the thought!" (Job 19:25–27).

My friend LeeAnn's forty-three-year-old husband died suddenly and unexpectedly of an aneurysm, leaving her with three young sons and a business to run. Later, as she read the book of Job, she wondered about Job's wife's comment. LeeAnn said, "I could never do that! Why would I curse the only hope I have left?" Only He has the words of eternal life; only in Him is there hope.

Oswald Chambers wrote this about the book of Job: "If the study of the Book of Job is making us reverent with what we don't understand, we are gaining insight. There is suffering before which you cannot say a word; you cannot preach 'the gospel of temperament'; all you can do is to remain dumb and leave room for God to come in as He likes. The point for us is—Do I believe in God apart from my reasoning about Him?"[7]

There is much we do not know. The life of Job reminds me that we're unaware of the battle going on in the spiritual realm. Job was not in on the conversation between God and Satan, and he was not happy about his suffering: "Is this not the struggle of all humanity? . . . I hate my life. I do not want to go on living" (Job 7:1, 16 TLB). Although Job had no clue why he was going through what he was going through, he held on to his faith.

A. W. Tozer understood the fear and confusion that comes with loss. He also understood exactly where to go for comfort.

Fear is the painful emotion that arises at the thought that we may be harmed or made to suffer. This fear persists while we are subject to the will of someone who does not desire our well-being. The moment we come under the protection of one of good will, fear is cast out. A child lost in a crowded store is full of fear because it sees the strangers around it as enemies. In its mother's arms a moment later all the terror subsides. The known good will of the mother casts out fear . . . to know that love is of God and to enter into the secret place leaning upon the arm of the Beloved—this and only this can cast out fear.[8]

Climb up in your Father's lap. Allow Him to hold you as you cry out your questions. Lay aside your fear as you rest in His loving embrace.

> *Come to Me, all you that labor and are heavy laden,*
> *and I will give you rest.*
> —MATTHEW 11:28

Set Aside Time to Grieve

This is the part I'd just as soon skip—the mourning. But we must not miss this important part of loss. Jesus said, "Blessed are they that mourn, for they shall be comforted" (Matthew 5:4). Mourning is the path to comfort. (At the end of this chapter, you'll find some specific helps on how to do the grief work.) When I was twenty-nine, my father died of cancer. My mother was also ill at the time and undergoing chemotherapy. I somehow thought I had to be strong for her—doing music for Dad's memorial service here in Oregon and in Montana—and I just did not take the time to do the work of grieving my father. Not many years after, I experienced deep depression and illness.

> Mourning is the path to comfort.

Everyone expresses grief differently, and you must be patient with yourself as you process it. The depression that struck Jason Clark at the height of his success as a pastor took time to work through. He needed this time to come to terms with how his childhood abuse affected him. Grief is work—work that we sometimes postpone, because feeling the loss is painful.

Flora Wuellner writes eloquently about the need to grieve:

Strangely enough, it is often hard to face the fact that we *are* suffering. Sometimes the pain is so chronic that we have grown accustomed to it. Sometimes we are numbed and anesthetized. Sometimes we have pushed ourselves so quickly into a positive response that we do not allow ourselves to feel the pain. Perhaps we try too quickly to forgive and forget or feel that our suffering is trivial or that we have no right to register suffering. Often it is with a sense of shock that we realize we *are* grieving and that we may have been carrying unhealed wounds for a long time. This often happens with those in the helping professions who are so used to themselves in the role of comforter and supporter that they become unaware of their own feelings and needs.[9]

Grieving is an important season in loss. It hurts to lose a loved one. It hurts terribly. But grieving your loss honors what you've lost and helps you to move on when it's time. Mourning is not a time for preaching lessons. It is a time for tears. It is a time to recognize and cherish what you had and lost, or a time to acknowledge what you never had.

> Grieving your loss honors what you've lost and helps you to move on when it's time.

The grieving path is one we must travel in order to finally come out of the dark valley. On that path we find that through the tears, the venting, and the anger, the old song is still true: "Where could I go, O where could I go? Needing a comfort for the soul . . . Where could I go but to the Lord?" Only He has the words of eternal life.

For the LORD will not cast off forever.
Though He causes grief, Yet He will show compassion
according to the multitude of His mercies.
For He does not afflict willingly, nor grieve the children of men.
—LAMENTATIONS 3:31–33

Remember to Breathe

While going through difficult times, it's *physically* important to breathe. When we are stressed, we tend to take shorter, shallow breaths, and even hold our breath, which can decrease the flow of oxygen to the body, making it harder to cope with stress. Practice taking abdominal breaths, deep breaths. The week Amy's baby was born, a friend called to remind me to breathe. My first reaction was, *What? I need to be reminded to breathe?* But it was some of the most helpful advice I received that week.

We live close to the most beautiful river in the world, the Metolius River. It bursts forth from underground a few miles from my home in central Oregon and flows for about thirty miles until it reaches Lake Billy Chinook. This river faces a lot of obstacles: it comes from snowmelt high in the Cascade mountain range and forces its way through rocks and miles of underground channels before it emerges—clean, sparkling, crystal clear, and icy cold.

It is so pure and clear you can see the rocks on the bottom of the river, along with the rainbow trout and kokanee (elusive to the persistent fly fishermen on the shores). During the months before Amy's baby was born, I would walk along the river, meditating on these verses:

This I recall to my mind,
Therefore I have hope.
Through the *LORD's* mercies we are not consumed,
Because His compassions fail not.
They are new every morning;

Great is Your faithfulness.
The LORD is my portion," says my soul,
"Therefore I hope in Him!"

(LAMENTATIONS 3:23–24)

As I walked along the river and looked up into the sky, I
thought of David's psalm of praise for God's mercy: "As the heavens
are high above the earth, so great is His mercy" (Psalm 103:11). I
realized that just as we breathe in oxygen for our existence, we can
breathe in His mercy. As Shakespeare reminded us centuries ago,
mercy is in the atmosphere!

> The quality of mercy is not strain'd,
> It droppeth as the gentle rain from heaven
> Upon the place beneath.
> It is twice bless'd:
> It blesseth him that gives and him that takes.[10]

Mercy—a fresh supply daily—is available. We can simply
breathe it in.

My friend Caro, who went through breast cancer, succeeding
treatments, and complications with chronic pneumonia, was sustained by an ancient prayer written by St. Teresa of Avila. Caro
breathed this ancient prayer meditatively, repeatedly:

> Let nothing disturb you;
> Nothing frighten you;
> All things are passing;
> God never changes;
> Patient endurance attains all things
> Whoever possesses God, lacks nothing;
> God alone suffices.[11]

Breathe this prayer or write your own. It is a wonderful tool to keep
you centered.

How do you recover from a broken heart? Maybe never, really. And yet Oswald Chambers pointed out,

> Why shouldn't we go through heartbreaks? Through those doorways God is opening up ways of fellowship with His son. . . . He comes with the pierced hand of His son, and says—"Enter into fellowship with Me." . . . If through a broken heart God can bring His purposes to pass in the world, then thank Him for breaking your heart.[12]

Although we may never be the same after a significant loss, Scripture assures us, "He heals the brokenhearted and binds up their wounds" (Psalm 147:3 LB). Life does go on. We cultivate an eye for the eternal, not the temporary. Perspective sharpens as we learn to cherish what is most important in life.

> *The LORD is merciful and gracious,*
> *Slow to anger, and abounding in mercy.*
> *He will not always strive with us,*
> *Nor will He keep His anger forever.*
> *He has not dealt with us according to our sins,*
> *nor punished us according to our iniquities.*
> *For as the heavens are high above the earth,*
> *So great is His mercy toward those who fear Him;*
> *As far as the east is from the west,*
> *So far has He removed our transgressions from us.*
> *As a father pities his children,*
> *so the LORD pities those who fear Him.*
> *For He knows our frame; He remembers that we are dust.*
> —Psalm 103:8–14

PERSONAL REFLECTION

Read chapters 6 and 7 of the book of Job. In these two chapters, Job tells honestly of his grief. Can you relate to any of his words in these two chapters? If so, which ones?

- Now read Job 13:13–10 (this is when Job answers his critics). Did you ever feel judged in your own loss, by others or by yourself? How have you responded?
- In Job 19:25–27, Job makes a triumphant statement of faith. How do his words inspire you?
- Read Job 23:2–12. What has been the effect of suffering upon Job? How does his example give you hope in your circumstances?

Take time to honor your loss by giving it the space and recognition that it deserves.

NEW BEGINNINGS RESOURCE

Soul Care Principles

Dr. Bill Gaultiere, of Christian Soul Care, offers several principles to help you work through your grief:[13]

1. Consider the year after your loss as a "season of grief," a time to cycle through important dates and memories and to progress through the stages of grief.

2. Get help from a grief recovery support group, pastor, or psychotherapist.

3. Take the initiative to talk about your grief over and over again with people you trust. (Don't feel sorry for yourself or isolate yourself if people seem to be avoiding you. This is simply due to their embarrassment of not knowing what to say.)

4. Feel your feelings and reminisce over your memories. When your grief is triggered by associations relating to your loved one (i.e., special dates, places, experiences, songs, smells), go with grief—as long as you're in a safe place.

5. Facilitate your grief recovery by doing things like revisiting the grave site or the place where the deceased's ashes were disbursed, listening to a tape of the memorial service, reminiscing over past memories and associations, and reviewing old pictures and memorabilia.

6. Write and share with a support person a letter or a series of letters to your loved one and/or to God to help you sort through your feelings.

7. Pray and read the Psalms for comfort (Psalm 3, 7, 13, 25, 44, 77, and 88).

And now my heart is broken. Depression
haunts my days. My weary nights are
filled with pain as though something were
relentlessly gnawing at my bones.

Job 30:16 NLT

CHAPTER THREE

After the Cards Stop Coming

IN CRISIS WE are often carried by adrenaline and by those around us. But it's the *after*—after you carefully package away the pain; after you put away the cards, the clippings, the remembrances. After people quit calling you, asking how you are. It's after you've gotten through some of the "firsts"—the birthdays, the holidays with an empty place at the table. Or it's after you've made it past your crisis, and you are trying to get used to the new normal, trying to cope with the new reality of a chronic health condition or adjusting to a major financial loss. Disappointment lingers like a bitter taste in your mouth.

And then we go on. We may not want to, but life pulls us back to living. Bills must be paid, meals must be shopped for and prepared, family and friends must be considered. In *afterloss*, you go through the motions. People used to call it "duty"—doing what must be done even if you don't feel like it.

It is during this time that we are especially vulnerable to depression, and it can make a home in us, descending like a bad cold when our immune system is down.

My friend Sherry Perrigan unexpectedly lost her husband, Steve, owing to complications from an illness. She says, "The first year was a blur. Sleep was difficult. I was not prepared for the actual, physical pain of losing Steve, my childhood sweetheart. My heart literally felt as if it were cut in half. I could not, *not* grieve." But after the first year, Sherry realized there was a point when people around her needed her to get better. She said, "So I smiled. I chose to be happy. But I'd go home and cry."

What do you do in this dreary place? First, understand that it's normal to suffer depression after you've experienced a loss or after a prolonged period of stress. Victor Parachin observes, "Many people report that the second year of bereavement is more difficult than the first. There are many reasons for this, including the fact that people are numb and in shock during the first weeks and months after a death. Again, be patient and do not expect overnight recovery. Try reminding yourself that others have recovered from their grief, and you will too, in your own time."[1]

Some of us are more prone to depression than others. I struggle with depression at times, and can relate to the "black dog" that Winston Churchill described and that Jason Clark related to in Chapter One. Depression is that nonspecific, dead weight that feels like a heavy, wet blanket. It can be a trying, colorless place. (I must also add here that depression can be caused by a variety of factors, including a chemical imbalance or can be a symptom of a physical or mental condition. It's important to get a good medical check-up to determine the cause of your depression. There are notes at the end of this chapter that suggest ways to know when you should get help.)

Trying to Make Sense of Things

There is a wonderful story in Luke 24 about two of Jesus' disciples. After Jesus' death, two disciples from Emmaus left Jerusalem to go back home, a seven-mile walk. As they walked, they talked, trying to make sense of what had happened.

Imagine how they felt in those immediate days after Jesus' death. Not understanding He would be resurrected, they felt sorrow and dismay. A bleak sense of loss and unanswered questions hung over them, as everything they had believed in had fallen apart. *How could they have gotten it so wrong? How could they go on?*

And what could it mean that Jesus' tomb was empty, as some of Jesus' women followers had discovered that morning? As they traveled they noticed a man walking beside them, and they began talking with him. Scripture says, "Their eyes were restrained, so that they did not know Him. And He said to them, 'What kind of conversation is this that you have with one another as you walk and are sad?'

Our unanswered question hangs in the air: *Why?*

"Then the one whose name was Cleopas answered and said to Him, 'Are You the only stranger in Jerusalem, and have You not known the things which happened there in these days?'" (Luke 24:18).

The two disciples told the stranger everything that had happened; they poured it all out. And then the stranger—Jesus—said to them, " 'O foolish ones, and slow of heart to believe in all that the prophets have spoken! Ought not the Christ to have suffered these things and to enter into His glory?' And beginning at Moses and all the Prophets, He opened all the Scriptures to them concerning Himself" (Luke 24:27).

It was getting dark when they reached Emmaus, and the two urged their fellow traveler to stay with them. So Jesus did. Scripture says that "as He sat at the table with them, He took bread, blessed and broke it, and gave it to them. Then their eyes were opened and they knew Him, and He vanished from their sight. And they said to one another, 'Did not our heart burn within us while He talked with us on the road, and while He opened the Scriptures to us?'"(Luke 24:16–32).

Something about this story captivates me. I can relate to Cleopas; maybe you can, too. We can feel abandoned and disappointed in God after a loss. His seeming absence can be almost palpable, encompassing. Our unanswered question hangs in the air: *Why?*

It seems to us that the world should stop going around, that the sun should stop shining; but it doesn't, so we plod on. I find it amazing that while Cleopas and the other disciple walked beside Jesus, pouring their hearts out to Him, they did not recognize Him! How was that possible?

Not long ago, I was at the gym, working out. I had been pounding on a treadmill for forty minutes before I saw that the person running next to me was a close friend. Why didn't I recognize her? Most likely because it took all I had to keep going on that treadmill! But it was also because I was in my own world. We can be in our own world of disappointment and grief and be unaware of God's loving presence. All the while we're pouring our hearts out to Him, we don't feel Him or see Him. It's the dark night of the soul.

Recently published letters by Mother Teresa reveal that, for most of her life, she felt abandoned by Christ and referred to Jesus as "the Absent One," calling her own smile "a mask." Although there were brief times of her life when she experienced the Presence of Christ, for most of her life, she was in the dark night of the soul. She wrote in 1961, "I have come to love the darkness for I believe now that it is part of a very, very small part of Jesus' darkness and pain on earth." She identified with Jesus' cry on the cross, "My God . . . Why have You forsaken me?"[2]

As the two disciples from Emmaus walked and talked, they tried to make sense of things, to sort them out. And don't we do the same? We try to make sense of our experience; we analyze it: *Where did we get it wrong? What could we have done to prevent this? What did we miss? Whose fault was it?* We can have feelings of failure, regret, and blame. And just plain sorrow. There's a risk to analysis, though. Joseph F. Schmidt writes, "We are aware that by judging an experience we have classified its importance and therefore controlled its impact. In the process of labeling, we have surrendered to the analysis of the ego and have manipulated our experience."[3]

> In other words, not so fast with the analysis.

In other words, not so fast with the analysis. Wait. Look for Jesus in this place. The One who promised never to leave us nor forsake us will show up.

From the end of the earth I will cry to You,
when my heart is overwhelmed;
Lead me to the rock that is higher than I.
—PSALM 61:2

Open Your Eyes to Shining Treasures

Perhaps one of the messages from Luke, chapter 24, is that, while we're experiencing *afterloss*, we can discover three unexpected, shining treasures offered to us from the risen Lord: we can gain a new vision of *true love, the preciousness of life*, and *the big picture*. But in order to find these priceless treasures, we must do one of those obvious things that we sometimes overlook—we must open our eyes.

Open Your Eyes to True Love

On the Emmaus walk, Jesus showed true love to his friends by simply showing up to be with them as they walked, and by listening to them. Listening is a profound way to show love. It has been said that the greatest gift we can give someone is to listen, because when we feel heard we feel loved.

My friend and I sat on the back deck of my house. We'd been friends since we'd had our babies together, years and miles ago. But on this day we were grieving together over my friend's recent divorce. She had poured her life into supporting her husband and had worked hard to help him succeed. Now she faced the reality of his extramarital affairs, and she wept bitter tears. "How could I have been so gullible? I worked so hard to make him look good. For *what?*"

The pain of the betrayal was deep. I had no words of advice for her, but I tried to listen. In the few days we had, we hiked in our beautiful mountains, we laughed, and we cried. The good news is that now, several years later, she has found love in another marriage.

She is a loving mother and grandmother, and she and her new husband reach out to other couples who need second chances. But at that moment in her life on my back deck, there were no answers. Only tears and questions. I remember saying rather lamely at one point, "Well . . . nothing you do in the spirit of love is ever wasted." As I look back, I agree. Love is never wasted.

> Nothing you do in the spirit of love is ever wasted.

The world will try to pound the love out of us. And some of us seem to get pounded by life more than others. How we need the love that will never let us go, a love that will not disappoint us or abandon us. It is the love that our heavenly Father has for each of us, his beautiful and much-longed-for children. This is a love that is more than words on a page; it becomes the only thing that, after all is said and done, matters. It is so simple we stumble over it. Often do not see it. But in reality, *nothing* can separate us from this love:

> Who shall separate us from the love of Christ? Shall tribulation, or distress, or persecution, or famine, or nakedness, or peril, or sword? . . . Yet in all these things we are more than conquerors through Him who loved us. For I am persuaded that neither death nor life, nor angels nor principalities nor powers, nor things present nor things to come, nor height nor depth, nor any other created things, shall be able to separate us from the love of God which is in Christ Jesus our LORD (Romans 8:35–39).

Jesus said, "Greater love has no man than this, that a man lay down his life for his friends . . . I call you friends" (John 15:13, 15). Listening can be a way of "laying our lives down"—asking thoughtful questions and then truly listening. Not with the intent to answer, but to hear. On the road to Emmaus, Jesus walked beside his disciples, listening before he spoke.

When we're feeling sad and depressed, it's hard to listen, sometimes impossible. Shortly after Amy relinquished her baby, we spent some time with another couple. One evening they poured their hearts out to us about a personal matter. Many months later, our friend confided that he had not felt we listened to him—that we blew off his pain. Looking back, I realize that we were in our own world of pain at the time, and even though we heard him, we hadn't *heard* him. Healing came to us over time as we were able to be heard. When we experience God's healing and listening love, we can reach out of that to others. Meanwhile, we must be patient with our journey.

In the place of *afterloss*, it is healing to listen to God, to listen to what is going on inside of us, and then to find a place where we can be heard. How good it is to know that we are loved and heard by the Great Listener.

My mother somehow was able to love each of us seven children in individual ways. When we were small, she would occasionally scoop one of us up in her arms, look us in the face, and ask, "*What does it feel like to be you?*" She really wanted to know. She was interested, she cared. This is empathy—wanting to know what it is like to be in someone else's shoes. This is exactly what our Lord did: "For we do not have a High Priest who cannot sympathize with our weaknesses, but was in all points tempted as we are, yet without sin. Let us therefore come boldly to the throne of grace that we may obtain mercy and find grace to help in time of need" (Hebrews 4:15, 16).

Love can hurt when we lose someone we love. Some years ago, I wrote in my journal, "Mother died three weeks ago. I write that line, but it is still so hard to believe. How can she die? That woman of laughter, of music, and of poetry? Even in her declining state, she loved. I wonder, When you lose someone you love, someone who loves you, what happens to the love? Where does it go?"

Where does it go, indeed? Paul wrote: "And now abide faith, hope, love, these three; but the greatest of these is love" (1 Corinthians 13:13). We must remember that love *abides*. Love never fails.

To see true love is to see that He walks beside us on the

journey, as He did with the two from Emmaus—even if we can't see Him right then. And because He walks with us, we can walk beside others on the journey, listening, loving, inviting them to life, reminding them of things that are eternal.

> *Love is patient; love is kind.*
> *It does not envy, it does not boast, it is not proud.*
> *It is not rude, it is not self-seeking,*
> *it is not easily angered, it keeps no record of wrongs.*
> *Love does not delight in evil but rejoices with the truth.*
> *It always protects, always trusts, always hopes, always perseveres.*
> *Love never fails.*
> —1 CORINTHIANS 13:4–8 NIV

Open Your Eyes to the Preciousness of Life

Jonathan Swift wrote, "May you live all the days of your life."[4]

There is nothing like loss to remind us how precious life is. In *afterloss*, we can have a fresh urgency to savor the moments with our loved ones—*now*. Bill's cousin Stan recently lost his wife in a plane crash. Miraculously, Stan was thrown clear of the plane, the only one to survive. When Bill called to express his sympathy, Stan said, "Bill, do something for me, will you? Tonight, put your arms around your wife and tell her you love her." Loss reminds us that life is precious. The poet T. S. Eliot wrote, "You are the music while the music lasts."[5]

> Because He walks with us, we can walk beside others on the journey.

We can wonder, *Where is my life? What happened to it?* When Mary came to the tomb looking for Jesus, the angel of the Lord asked her, "Why do you seek the living among the dead?" (Luke 24:5). In our most depressing days, we may have to be intentional about looking for life.

My friend and her husband had been going through trying

times. Although they did not have children at home, it was Valentine's Day, and they strongly felt the need for some life in their house. They called their neighbors, a young couple with two small children, and asked if they could borrow their children for a Saturday. What a great time they had, making Valentine cookies and Valentines for the children's parents. When they took the children back home, their house was a mess, but they were happy. They took time on an ordinary Saturday to taste the preciousness of *life*, and they found it.

The two disciples' eyes were opened when Jesus broke the bread and blessed it. He said, "I am the bread of life" (John 6:35). In the breaking of bread, we partake of life. It is significant that we bring food to people when they have had a loss. Maybe the message is, "You are still living. You must eat; gather strength to go on." Robert Browning wrote, "You never know what life means till you die; even throughout life, 'tis death that makes life live."[6]

Invest in life. Look to renew old dreams and make new plans. Be creative in turning your loss into gain. On both of my parents' birthdays, I do something to honor their memory. For instance, one year on my dad's birthday (because he was so good at caring for people), I did a project to help a family in need.

Great pain can release great energy to touch others with compassion. Mothers Against Drunk Driving (MADD) is a nonprofit organization that was started in 1980 by Candice Lightner after her thirteen-year-old daughter was killed by a drunk driver. MADD has grown into a successful national organization that has helped to pass legislation and heighten awareness of drunk driving. And the death rate from alcohol-related traffic accidents has declined from 26,173 in 1982 to 16,885 in 2005, largely because of the efforts of MADD.[7]

> Great pain can release great energy to touch others with compassion.

Sherry Tucker and her husband, Dirk, who lost their son Zachary to brain cancer, have started a foundation called Giving Hope Through Faith Foundation, with the primary purpose of sharing the love of Christ with families experiencing the trials of cancer.

Intentionally investing in life in the midst of our own pain helps bring healing.[8]

J. W. Follette wrote,

> The one who has had but little trouble in life is not a particularly helpful person. But one who has gone through a hundred and one trials, experiences, deaths, blasted hopes, shocks, and a tragedy or two and has learned his lesson. . . . Such a person is worthwhile. He is able to enter into the need of suffering humanity and pray it through. He can enter into perfect fellowship with a person who is in unspoken agony of spirit and pressure of trial. He is able to look beyond the frailty of flesh and, remembering we are but dust, to trust God with a sublime faith for victory and power. Do not be afraid of the process. I see such rich possibilities in it all. We long to be of service to needy mankind. Nothing can better equip us than to break in spirit and heart and so become clear, sparkling wine, rich and refreshing.[9]

I am come that they may have life,
and that they may have it have it more abundantly.
—JOHN 10:10

Open Your Eyes to the Big Picture

Some time ago, our family was in our boat off the Washington coast. A storm came up, and we got caught in a gale. To make matters worse, the engine quit and the waves were pushing us toward jagged rocks. We panicked, trying everything we knew; we had on our life jackets. We radioed the Coast Guard for help, and they told us: *Put down your anchor!* We did, and were secured. Later, as we were being towed back to the harbor, we felt pretty silly that we hadn't thought of putting our anchor down first.

It's easy to panic in the midst of a storm. But it's in those times when we don't know what to do that we must walk out the truth that we do know and drop anchor into God's Word, where shifting sands and tides cannot touch. Hebrews 6:19 says, "This hope we have as an anchor of the soul, both sure and steadfast."

One morning our friend Rich was visiting his elderly mother. She was very ill, barely holding on to life. Rich gently asked her, "Mom, wouldn't you like to go be with the Lord? And see Dad?"

"Well, *yes . . .*" she replied. "But first I'd like to have breakfast." So, of course, he helped her get some breakfast! We are quite earthbound, aren't we? Earth is all we know, but Jesus gently encourages us to see beyond the crucifixion, beyond the resurrection to eternity.

Thomas Merton, in *No Man Is an Island*, gives us a view of the big picture, of life beyond this earth:

> Christianity is Christ living in us, and Christ has conquered everything. . . . His love is so much stronger than death that the death of a Christian is a kind of triumph. And although we rightly sorrow . . . we rejoice in their death because it proves to us the strength of our mutual love. This is our great inheritance . . . this grip of clean love that holds us so fast that it keeps us eternally free. This love, this life, this presence, is the witness that the spirit of Christ lives in us, and that we belong to Him, and that the Father has given us to Him, and no man shall snatch us out of His hand.[10]

On the road to Emmaus, when Jesus showed up and walked with the two disciples in their sorrow, in their questioning, he didn't immediately reveal himself to them and say, "Here I am—problem solved!" He let them talk it out. He listened to them. And then, after listening, he reminded them of what Scripture said. He directed them to see the big picture, to seek the eternal.

Investing in things that last means to believe the big picture, to believe that God's Word is true, that Jesus came to die for all, that He is not willing that any should perish, and that we are to love others as Christ loved us. This is the anchor that holds us when storms inevitably come.

When Brad and Susan were going through their financial meltdown, it seemed as if the bad news just kept coming. Together they struggled with feelings of regret and self-condemnation. They knew many others who were in the same situation, but knowing they weren't the only ones didn't help. At their ages, financial loss was devastating, and the recession they got caught in was like a tsunami, destroying everything they'd worked for. One afternoon Brad grabbed Susan in the kitchen and began dancing with her as he sang, "This world is not my home, I'm just a-passin' through. My treasures are laid up, somewhere beyond the blue!" Brad grinned at Susan's look of dismay, "Don't worry, Susan, it's just money!" She said later, "It is true—my inheritance is more than what I have here on earth. I just have to keep reminding myself of it."

C. S. Lewis wrote:

> If you read history, you will find that the Christians who did the most for the present world were just those who thought most of the next. The apostles themselves, who set on foot the conversion of the Roman Empire, the great men who built up the Middle Ages, the English evangelicals who abolished the slave trade, all left their mark on earth, precisely because their minds were occupied with heaven. It is since Christians have largely ceased to think of the other world that they have become so ineffective in this.[11]

This life is not all there is. It is a training ground; a place to learn the very few, important things in life about love, and cherishing what is essential and lasting.

We fix our eyes not on what is seen, but on what is unseen.
For what is seen is temporary, but what is unseen is eternal.
—2 CORINTHIANS 4:18

Scars—Marks of Identification

The two disciples from Emmaus were so excited to have seen Jesus that they immediately went back to Jerusalem to tell the other disciples. They said to each other, "Didn't our hearts feel strangely warm as he talked with us on the road and explained the Scriptures to us?" (Luke 24:32 NLT). It was dark. It was a seven-mile walk. But I'm sure they made great time. When they reached the other disciples, they told them how Jesus had appeared to them as they were walking along the road and how they had recognized him as he was breaking the bread. Just as they were telling about it, Jesus himself was suddenly standing there among them. Imagine their fright! Jesus said to them, "Why are you frightened? Why do you doubt who I am? Look at my hands. Look at my feet" (Luke 24:38, 39 NLT).

And Jesus presented the proof of who he was: the scars in his side, his hands, and feet. The scars were his marks of identification, proof that he was who he said he was.

J. R. Miller writes of the scars that sorrow produces:

> Sorrow makes deep scars; it writes its record ineffaceably on the heart which suffers. We really never get over our great griefs; we are never altogether the same after we had passed through them as we were before. Yet there is a humanizing and fertilizing influence in sorrow which has been rightly accepted and cheerfully borne. Indeed, they are poor who have never suffered and have none of sorrow's marks upon them. God has ordered that in pressing on in duty we shall find the truest, richest comfort for ourselves.[12]

My daughter, Amy, has a mysterious scar that completely encircles her left arm. We do not know what it's from. Amy used to make up stories about it. One story was that while she was fishing with her dad, he accidentally wound fishing line around her arm when he was casting. Another story she tells is that her birth mother did it so that years later, her mother could find her. Last summer, when Amy and I were in Korea, we asked various ones at the orphanage, the city hall, and at the adoption agency if they knew the origin of the scar. No one seemed to know. Amy used to be ashamed of it and hid it under long-sleeved shirts. Now she seems comfortable with it. Whatever it is, it is part of her; it is a mark of identification.

When Amy and I visited South Korea, we had three bits of information: we knew the city where she was born, the address where she was left, and the date of her birth. She was three months old when she was left with her birth date pinned to her.

We first visited the city of Gangneung, Amy's birthplace, with our guide and interpreter, Mr. Whang. He arranged for us to visit City Hall, and the officials there carried in a large record book and opened it to show Amy. Mr. Whang interpreted what we were seeing: Amy's birth date, August 2, 1980. And there was her mother's name, Cho Soon Ja. It was an emotional moment, to have a name: Soon Ja. We deducted then, that Yung Ja (Amy's Korean name) was possibly named after her mother, as Yung Ja means "Little One."

We then drove to another part of the city to find the address where Amy was left. The city, a beautiful sea resort, has changed dramatically in twenty-eight years. We wound through fields and back roads and finally came to an elegant, traditional Korean house.

"I think this is it," our guide said. We stood in front of it, wondering. Amy said that this was the answer to her prayers, to know where she came from. "No offense, Mom," Amy said, "you're my mom, but I have another mother."

"You absolutely do, Amy," I said. "Her blood flows through you." Later, Amy said, "The most powerful moment was to know I was probably named after my birth mother. I thought maybe the orphanage just named me. To see there was an actual record of *me* was wonderful. I was named by my birth mother! That made me feel blessed."

As I stood by the graveled road in front of the house, I thanked God for the gift that is my daughter, Amy. I thanked God for new life in beautiful little Annabelle. I thought of my loving husband and wonderful sons and daughters-in-law and my other amazing grandchildren, now so far away from the spot where I stood.

During the trip, I read and reread Romans 8—and realized in a fresh way that everything really is all about love. About not having the "spirit of bondage to fear" but the "spirit of adoption." And who can separate us from the love of Christ? Nothing! Not life, nor death. Not even a few continents or oceans, not nations or languages. Not even long nights of the soul.

I thought of the love Soon Ja had for her Yung Ja, our Amy—perhaps still has. How difficult her life had to be, to make the terrible decision to leave her daughter. Solomon wrote, "Many waters cannot quench love, nor can the floods drown it" (Song of Solomon 8:7).

Love never fails. Love abides. And in his good time, the Redeemer will make all things beautiful and someday there will be no more tears, no more paralyzing sadness, no more separations.

Mark Buchanan writes:

Our deepest instinct is heaven. Heaven is the ache in our bones, the splinter in our heart. Like the whisper of faraway waves we hear crashing in the whorls of a conch shell, the music of heaven echoes, faint, elusive, haunting, beneath and within our daily routines. . . . The instinct for heaven is just that: homesickness, ancient as night, urgent as daybreak. All your longings—for the place you grew up, for the taste of raspberry tarts that your mother once pulled hot from the oven, for that bend in the river where your father took you fishing as a child, where the water was dark and swirling and the caddis flies hovered in the deep shade—all these longings are a homesickness, a wanting in full what all these things only hint at, only prick you with. These are the things seen that conjure in our emotions the Things Unseen. "He has set eternity in the hearts of men," the writer of Ecclesiastes said; "yet they cannot fathom what God has done from beginning to end" (3:11).[13]

Jesus left this earth scarred, and so will we. He was wounded for our transgressions and, out of love for us, bears scars in His hands, His feet, and in His side. True love and eternal life is found in the One who knows no time, who put aside his glorious garment of light to take on the human form in order to communicate redeeming love to us, His children.

> *A man's days resemble grass.*
> *He blossoms like a flower in the field, the wind blows over it,*
> *and it is gone with not a sign that it has been there.*
> *But the* LORD's *faithful love*
> *rests eternally upon those who revere Him*
> *and His righteousness on the children's children*
> *on those who re faithful to His covenant*
> *who remember to carry out His instructions.*
> —PSALM 103:15–18 *Berkeley*

PERSONAL REFLECTION

Read Luke 24. Notice that Jesus listened to the two disciples as they poured out their loss.

1. Do you feel listened to, in your own loss? Try to find a safe place to be heard by another person. (And, of course, remember that you can always pour out your honest prayers to God. He is the ultimate "safe place"!)

2. From your recent experience, what important lessons have you learned about love?

3. Think of some practical, hands-on ways you can affirm *life*.

4. Write down what you are learning about the Big Picture. How can you invest in things that last?

NEW BEGINNINGS RESOURCE

When to Seek Help for Depression

We all feel sad, lonely, or depressed at times. Occasional episodes of feeling this way are normal, and it is certainly normal after a major loss. But when the depression does not pass or is severe, you need help. If depression is negatively affecting your life—such as causing difficulties with relationships, work issues, or family disputes—and there isn't a clear solution to these problems, seek help, especially if these feelings persist for any length of time.

The diagnosis of depression begins with a physical exam by a doctor. There are certain viruses, medicines, and illnesses that can cause depression-like symptoms, and it's important to have a thorough exam by a physician to make a proper diagnosis.

Signs and Symptoms of Depression

- Difficulty concentrating, remembering details, and making decisions

- Fatigue and decreased energy

- Feelings of guilt, worthlessness, and/or helplessness

- Insomnia, early-morning wakefulness, or excessive sleeping

- Irritability, restlessness

- Loss of interest in activities or hobbies once pleasurable, including sex

- Overeating or appetite loss

- Persistent aches or pains, headaches, cramps, or digestive problems that do not ease with treatment

- Thoughts of suicide, suicide attempts

Depression carries a risk of suicide. Anybody who expresses suicidal thoughts or intentions should be taken very, very seriously. If you or someone you know is having suicidal thoughts or feelings, seek help immediately from a professional, a physician, psychiatrist, psychologist, or pastor. Help is available. Do not hesitate to call your local suicide hotline immediately. Call 1-800-784-2433 or 1-800-273-8255.

Warning Signs of Suicide[14]

- A sudden switch from being very sad to being very calm or appearing happy

- Always talking or thinking about death

- Clinical depression that gets worse

- Having a "death wish," tempting fate by taking risks that could lead to death

- Losing interest in things one used to care about

- Putting affairs in order, tying up loose ends, changing a will

- Saying things like "it would be better if I wasn't here," or "I want out"

- Talking about suicide (killing one's self)

- Visiting or calling people one cares about

PART TWO

Spiritual Strategies to Lead You to a New Beginning

O God, who is like You?
You, who have shown me great and severe troubles,
shall revive me again . . . You shall . . . comfort me on every side.
—Psalm 71:19b, 20, 21

He had a word, too. Love, he called it.
But I had been used to words for a long time.
I knew that that word was like the others:
just a shape to fill a lack.

—William Faulkner[1]

CHAPTER FOUR

Spiritual Strategy #1: Release the Healing Power of Words

WHEN WE'RE IN serious pain, finding any words at all may be impossible. And when we do speak to ourselves, we often end up saying words of condemnation or criticism. Words have great power—for good or for harm. Words are tools, and the power of words is how we use them. And while words may not change the truth of our situation, the words we use can help us heal.

Each one of us is a word spoken by God. Created in His image, we have the power to create with our words. Our words can create an atmosphere of faith or fear. Some words create more pain; the lack of words can even delay healing. We can choose words of affirmation or condemnation. Solomon wrote, "Death and life *are* in the power of the tongue" (Proverbs 18:21).

Some words stay with us for a lifetime, sustaining us. Certain psalms, scripture verses, hymns, or poetry that we memorized as children come back to us. These words speak to deep places within, comforting us and giving us hope for the future. Yesterday I walked into a gift shop and heard a CD playing in the background: "'Tis so sweet to trust in Jesus . . ." As I browsed among the scented candles and gift books, the words carried me back to thoughts of my Grandmother Olson. That was her favorite hymn. She was widowed in the Great Depression and raised four children without benefit of social security. She suffered many losses and struggled just to feed her family. To her, "trusting in Jesus" was not mere words. It was a forceful truth that carried her and her family, and they eventually thrived and overcame their poverty.

Tell Yourself the Truth about Your Truth

For healing to begin, it's important to see the truth of our experience, to put words to it. When you are ready, find a safe place to begin to deal with your loss or your difficult situation. It may be helpful for you to journal these things in a notebook that is yours alone. It may work best for you to enter your thoughts on your computer. You may be the kind of person who needs to talk it out with someone else, such as a counselor, a pastor, or a trusted friend. You may benefit from being in a grief recovery group, something many people find helpful. Or you may need all of these tools to help in your healing.

> For healing to begin, it's important to see the truth of our experience.

When Gingir Hakala lost her husband, Don, people gave her books to read. But initially she found it hard to even concentrate enough to read. She talked out her grief with a counselor, and also went to a grief recovery group that helped her. She says that when she was able to read, "the Psalms were the most comforting, so that's what I read."

If you think journaling might be a helpful avenue for you, consider what kind of journal you'd like to use. I like using a spiral-bound, throw-away notebook. Sometimes it's easier to be gut-level honest when you know you can throw away certain pages if necessary. But a nice, pretty journal may be best for you. Or maybe you prefer to use a document in your computer. Whatever works best for you, here are some questions you can ask yourself to get you started:

- What do I hurt most about?
- What happened to cause this wound?
- How has this wound affected me?

Then, as you continue to journal and process your thoughts, you can ask yourself:

- Why is this still causing me pain?
- What is the status of my healing? Am I making progress?
- What am I learning from my pain and from my healing?
- What are some things I can let go of?

Then, find scriptures that counteract your negative feelings and write them down. Read them often. Meditate on them. Memorize them.

Whatever method of expression works best for you, be honest about your experience, your own self, and your own conflicted emotions: write it, journal it, talk about it, cry it out. Yes, you may have been victimized by another's negative choices, but have the courage to see your own weaknesses and your own rage and frustration. It takes courage to see the truth. But as Douglas Steere writes, "Saints . . . are ordinary people who are inwardly attending to the highest truth they know and who are prepared to let this truth have undivided sway in their lives. . . . [They] are not afraid of consequences because they are such avid lovers of the truth they have found."[2]

The truth may be painful to face, but *not* facing it is much more painful. Buried wounds fester and become infected. Jesus told us long ago: "You shall know the truth, and the truth shall make you free" (John 8:32).

In the remainder of this chapter, I'll be sharing several words from God. His Word will have a powerful impact on your life as you soak it in and allow it to become a part of you.

> *Behold, You desire truth in the inward parts,*
> *and in the hidden part You will make me to know wisdom.*
> —PSALM 51:6

Apply Scripture to Your Truth

While it's important to be honest about our pain or negative circumstances, it's possible to get stuck in our pain, become absorbed in it. The children of Israel were very honest about their pain while wandering in the wilderness. They had complaining honed to a fine art. The reason they couldn't leave the wilderness was that they did not hear or obey God's voice to them *while* in the wilderness.

> While it's important to be honest about our pain or negative circumstances, it's possible to get stuck in our pain.

God's Word is living and powerful and we can apply its truth to our circumstances: "He sent His Word and He healed them, and delivered them from their destructions" (Psalm 107:20).

One night shortly before Amy's baby was born, I tossed and turned in bed. It looked like it would be another sleepless night, agonizing over the thought of Amy relinquishing her baby. We agreed with her decision, but it was so hard. I prayed, "God, I simply cannot bear this." I finally got out of bed and went to my chair in the living room and grabbed my Bible, searching for something to give me peace. The words from Isaiah 53 leaped out at me: "Surely I have borne your griefs and carried your sorrows." It seemed the Lord was saying, "You do not have to bear it. I already have. Let me carry all of you through this." The truth of these words from Isaiah gave me peace, and I was able to sleep.

In my book *Desperate for God*, I tell about Sue Stanley, who went through a series of devastating losses.[3] Her parents died in the spring of 1990 in a murder-suicide. A year later, her husband left her. Within a short period of time, she was an orphan and a single mom, trying to comfort herself and her children in their losses. She was not sure how she could go on, but she told me how God met her in (of all places) a movie theater.

Her son Brian was four, and she was taking him to the movies for the first time, going with her neighbors. On the way, the neighbor's all-knowing five-year-old daughter told Brian that the theater was dark, and he probably wouldn't like it. They got there, bought their tickets, and were laden with popcorn and treats when Brian balked. Everyone else had gone in, but Brian stood at the door and wailed, "No, no, no!"

Sue told me that as she leaned down to talk to her sobbing son, the Lord whispered to her in a still, small voice, "Sue, what you are going to say to Brian I am going to say to you."

She found herself saying, "Honey, I know it's dark in there, and I know you're scared, but I brought you here because I know something you don't know. I've been here before, and I know what it's like in there. There's something really good in there, and I know you'll like it, but you can't see it unless you go in."

> "Honey, I know it's dark in there, but I brought you here because I know something you don't know."

Sue said that as she was speaking, she immediately thought of Jeremiah 29:11: "I know the plan I have for you, plans to prosper you and not to harm you." She continued, "I'm not sending you in there alone. I'll be with you and hold your hand, and I won't let go." She thought of Isaiah 41:10: "So do not fear, for I am with you; do not be dismayed, for I am your God. I will strengthen you and help you; I will uphold you with my righteous right hand."

Sue said Brian grew calmer and began listening to her. She then had a further inspiration. She poked her head into the dark theater, came back and said, "Brian, it's only dark in this little hallway. Around the corner there are little lights on the floor, lights on the walls, and lots more light from the screen." She knew she was talking about the little lights in her life—the strategic people God had sent as comforters and advisers, who brought her joy and laughter in the midst of unbelievable pain. And the best light of all—Jesus Himself: "The Lord is my light and my salvation!" (Psalm 27:1).

Finally convinced, Brian looked up at his mother, took her hand, tucked his popcorn under one arm, and walked into the theater with her. When they sat down next to their friends, Sue's neighbor asked where they'd been. All Sue could manage was, "I just had an encounter with the living God in the lobby!"

Remember the Word to Your servant,
upon which You have caused me to hope.
This is my comfort, in my affliction,
for Your Word has given me Life.
—PSALM 119:49, 50

Pray Honest Prayers

Many of the Psalms are prayers. Honest, venting prayers! God is a big God, and He can handle our honesty. W. H. Auden wrote, "It is where we are wounded that God speaks to us."[4] We don't like being in those wounded places. Pain makes us uncomfortable, and it makes us feel out of control, weak. And yet it is in our pain that we most need to hear Him.

Pray honest prayers. Share your deepest pains and doubts with God. It may be helpful for you to write down, or journal, your prayers, your questions for God. God can handle our anger questions.

> Pray honest prayers. Share your deepest pains and doubts with God.

When you do call out to God and seek His help, He has promised that He will answer: " 'Then you will call upon Me and come and pray to Me, and I will listen to you. You will seek Me and find Me when you search for Me with all your heart. I will be found by you,' declares the LORD" (Jeremiah 29:12–14 NASB).

The writer of Hebrews tells us to come to Him in faith: "He who comes to God must believe that He is; and that He is a rewarder of them that diligently seek Him" (Hebrews 11:6). Our faith may be shaky, and we may pray like the father of the sick child in the Bible, "LORD, I believe, help my unbelief!" (Mark 9:24). Our faith can be as tiny as a mustard seed. What matters is that we come to Him with our whole, honest selves—worries, insecurities, rage, doubts and all. I love *The Message* version of Psalm 30:2: "God, my God, I yelled for help, and you put me together. God, you pulled me out of the grave, gave me another chance at life when I was down and out."

Pray out your thoughts and fears. God already knows the truth of your pain, but as you pray it out to Him, His healing balm will begin to fill your heart.

> *And it shall come to pass, that before they call,*
> *I will answer; and while they are still speaking, I will hear.*
> —ISAIAH 65:24

Take Time to Be Still

Whether our days are hectic with all the business of life or they drag on in emptiness and loneliness, it is essential that we stop and take time to be still and be with God. It is in our silence that we will encounter the presence of God. Henri Nouwen wrote,

> It is in our silence that we will encounter the presence of God.

> Out of eternal silence God spoke the Word, and through this Word created and recreated the world. In the beginning God spoke the land, the sea, and the sky. God spoke the sun, the moon, and the stars. God spoke plants, birds, fish, animals wild and tame. Finally, God spoke man and woman. Then

in the fullness of time, God's Word, through whom all had been created, became flesh and gave power to all who believe to become the children of God. In all this, the Word of God does not break the silence of God, but rather unfolds the immeasurable richness of that silence. . . . A word with power is a word that comes out of silence.[5]

We hear God when we dare to be silent: *Be still, and know . . .* (Psalm 42:10)

Being out in nature is a way to be still with God, and it is healing. Take time to be outside, to look up into the sky and wonder. Look around you and savor the beauty of the trees, flowers, and plants. God speaks to us through the majesty of His creation.

Missionary Amy Carmichael, who spent fifty-six years in India in the latter part of the 1800s and early 1900s, reminds us to open our eyes: "Look again at this bare bush. Look at the delicate tracery of its shadow-lines on the snow. The sun is shining behind the bush and so every little twig is helping to make something that is very beautiful . . . the spring will come again, for after winter there is always spring. But when? . . . I do not know. I only know that sun and snow are working together for good. . . . He will not fail you, who is the God of the sun and the snow."[6]

Amy saw the evidence of God in nature when she took time to be still with Him. David declared the same thing in the psalms: "The heavens declare the glory of God; and the firmament shows His handiwork. Day unto day utters speech, and night unto night reveals knowledge. *There is* no speech nor language *where* their voice is not heard" (Psalm 19:1–3).

Try to set some time aside each day to simply sit quietly with God. You might read a passage of scripture or listen to some praise music to get you in the right frame of mind; but then, stop. Be quiet. Take some time to listen. Judge and Amy Reinhold have compiled a beautiful book titled *Be Still*. It includes entries by writers such as Max Lucado, Henry Cloud, Philip Yancey, and many more. Scriptures, quotes, meditations—all chosen to teach you how to have a "Be Still" experience with God. This is just one tool that can help guide you as you learn to be still with God.

> *Be still, and know that I am God;*
> *I will be exalted among the nations, I will be exalted in the earth!*
> *The Lord of hosts is with us; The God of Jacob is our refuge.*
> —PSALM 42:10

Recite Words of Faith

The words you speak to yourself significantly affect how you think and feel—even what you believe. There's an old saying attributed to F. F. Bosworth, "Believe your beliefs and doubt your doubts." We can choose to focus more on possibilities and the good things that can happen than on despair and the bad things that can happen. We can choose to make statements of faith, rather than statements of fear. We can rehearse what we have, rather than what we do not have.

> We can choose to make statements of faith, rather than statements of fear.

My friend Kay tells about the time when her teenaged son ran away. She says, "Fortunately I had been praying with some of my friends, and I went to my knees in faith, believing he would be found. The words 'five days' came to my mind." She said that holding on to those words was better than worrying—which is like being in a rocking chair, going back and forth and back and forth, but going nowhere! Their son did come home in five days, and he was fine. The words of faith that she chose to repeat to herself helped her endure those five difficult days.

Speaking, hearing words of faith keeps us going, builds our faith. When my husband was going through a trial, a friend called and left a message on his cellphone: "Bill," she said, "while I was walking today, God gave me a word for you." And then there was silence. "Oh, my goodness! I forgot what that word was. I guess I'm having a senior moment. I'll call you back." Later she left another message: "Bill, I remembered what the word was: 'God will perfect that which concerns you.'" Bill laughed as he let me listen to the message, but it meant a lot to him.

One day Jesus was mobbed by crowds of people, wanting help from him. In the crowd was a woman who had had a flow of blood for twelve years. "When she heard about Jesus, she came behind Him in the crowd and touched His garment. For she said, 'If only I may touch His clothes, I shall be well.' Immediately she felt in her body that she was healed of the affliction. And Jesus, immediately knowing in Himself that power had gone out of Him, turned around in the crowd and said, 'Who touched My clothes?' . . . But the woman, fearing and trembling, knowing what had happened to her, came and fell down before Him and told Him the whole truth. And He said to her, 'Daughter, your faith has made you well. Go in peace, and be healed of your affliction'" (Mark 5:25–34).

Faith is powerful. Faith overcomes. This woman knew that Jesus was her last hope. She had tried everything else. But she persisted and pressed through the crowds to touch Him. We, too, can persist; we can press through the layers of years or time to touch Him, to receive healing for our wounds. Healing words are words of faith: "The Word of God is near you; it is in your mouth and in your heart" (Romans 10:8 NIV). We can speak and rehearse words of faith. Not presumptuous words—but words that agree with the truth of God's Word and the gift of faith He puts in our hearts.

> We can speak words that agree with the truth of God's Word and the gift of faith He puts in our hearts

Your faith has made you well. Go in peace.
—MARK 5:34 NLT

Hold On to Words of Hope

Hope is what carries us forward. Sherry Perrigan told me, "Twenty-some years ago I went through a very painful trauma. A close friend allowed me to pour out my heart, and when I had finished, she looked me right in the eye and said in truth—not judgmentally—that she didn't completely understand because she had never gone through anything like it. Then in love, she said, '*But there's hope.*' I'll never forget how that cut through to my troubled heart." Sherry says that as she looks back over this past year and the recent loss of her husband, "Above all else, I needed to feel there was hope. My friend's words over twenty years ago gave me hope this year. Hope that He would restore me. My friend gave me, through her words, a gift."

> "Above all else, I needed to feel there was hope."

George Herbert, a sixteenth-century preacher, wrote: "Good words are worth much, and cost little."[7] We can choose to say to ourselves and to hear words of hope.

One couple with a vibrant marriage of over thirty years confided that every day they make it a point to say something positive to one another—and make a point to forgive the negative. Small words can have an enormous impact.

Memorize words that give you hope. Read them. Think about them. Read hopeful stories of others who have gone through difficult times, and remember that you can survive, too.

My friend Mari Hanes tells of the time when she was a young pastor's wife with four children. She had looked forward to their denomination's convention for a year. But at the convention, her two little boys were sick with severe allergies, and their newly adopted tiny daughter from Bulgaria had arrived with myriad special problems. She found herself spending all of the time at the back of the auditorium in the restroom with her needy children. She didn't get to hear any of the Bible teaching she so wanted to soak in. She said, "One night, a respected and beloved friend, and the mother of four grown children, Mrs. Anna Hayford, came to the back of the auditorium where I was rocking a feverish child while my others cuddled nearby. She put her hand on my arm and said, 'Mari, it *does* get easier.' Then she patted my back and left. I did not get to hear a single teaching at that convention, but I went home with Anna's words in my heart: *It does get easier.* And those simple words of hope gave me strength."

The same is true for you, dear friend. It *does* get easier. Hold words of hope in your heart and allow them to carry you through. Dean Merrill writes:

> Hope and fear are thus like two ships passing in the night, but headed in opposite directions. They are at the same dark, murky point in the ocean. But by morning, they will be miles apart. Because hope keeps saying, "Well, it's possible." Hope just may blossom someday into something impressive like faith. That is why Hebrews 11:1 defines faith as "being sure of what we hope for." In the beginning we are not sure at all. We know too well that it is ridiculous to put hope in ourselves. We have already demonstrated our own shortcomings. We can only hope that God is wise enough to make something beautiful out of our messed-up lives. . . . People in trouble often say, "I don't want to get my hopes up." Yes! Get them up! The Scriptures promise in Romans 5:5 that "hope does not disappoint us, because God has poured his love into our hearts by the Holy Spirit, whom he has given us." We have good reason to hope . . . because hope is another word for confidence, and confidence in the Savior's work is all that is required.[8]

> *Hope does not disappoint, because the love of God*
> *has been poured out within our hearts*
> *through the Holy Spirit who was given to us.*
> —ROMANS 5:5 NASB

Be Sustained by Words of Comfort

When your heart is breaking, turn to God's Word for His overflowing comfort. Some of the most comforting words are those that God speaks directly to us in our pain: "As a mother comforts her child, so will I comfort you" (Isaiah 66:13 NIV).

God understands our pain more than we can ever know. He does not stand idly by as we agonize in our heart. No. He holds us as we cry. He hurts with us. He speaks words of comfort to us— just as a mother comforts her child.

One of the reasons Jesus became human was so He could walk this earth and understand how we feel. Being understood is a great comfort. The Hebrew writer says of Him: "For this reason he had to be made like his brothers in every way, in order that he might become a merciful and faithful high priest" (Hebrews 2:17 NIV).

Jesus—God in flesh—boldly speaks to us in our pain. His healing words comfort us, sustain us: "Neither do I condemn you, go and sin no more" (John 8:11). Jesus repeatedly said, "Don't be afraid." He said: "Be of good cheer; I have overcome the world" (John 16:33). He comforts us with: "I will never leave you nor forsake you" (Hebrews 13:5).

Comfort is both a gift that is given to us by others and a gift that we choose for ourselves. Just as a child has to finally "allow" his or her mother to offer comfort by accepting her arms of love and her words of encouragement, so we, too, must open our hearts to the words of comfort that are offered to us.

> *Blessed be the God and Father of our* LORD *Jesus Christ,*
> *the Father of mercies and God of all comfort,*
> *who comforts us in all our tribulation.*
> —2 CORINTHIANS 1:3

PERSONAL REFLECTION

Read Proverbs 18:21. Have you seen the impact of words upon your life? Take time to be aware of your own words—spoken and unspoken. Are they life-giving words?

1. Ask yourself, "Am I rehearsing healing words? Or do I tend to speak and think words of condemnation and defeat?"
2. Ask yourself, "What practical ways can I stop negative, defeating words?"

Read Jeremiah 15:16: "Your words were found, and I ate them . . ."

1. Find two or three other healing passages of Scripture that you can memorize and rehearse. Meditate upon them, counteracting words of hopelessness and despair.
2. Consider some creative ways to bring healing into your life through words (for instance, music, poetry, or journaling).

NEW BEGINNINGS RESOURCE

Where to Find Words of Comfort

Music can be wonderfully healing and uplifting. Praise music, the old hymns, and classical music can all fill the soul.

Poetry. While poetry can be intimidating, it can be very healing in times of trauma. Words are inadequate for some huge losses, and poetry can give us a language to speak the words we cannot.

I enjoy poetry by Edna St. Vincent Millay. I also recommend the small classical book of poetry, *One Hundred and One Famous Poems*. (See *The Eternal Goodness*, by John Greenleaf Whittier.)

Much of Psalms is poetry and touches the deep places within us as nothing else can. Take time to meditate upon these verses; repeat them. Personalize them (i.e., "God, Your grace is sufficient for me. Your strength is made perfect in my weakness.")

Recommended reading
A Grief Observed by C. S. Lewis
Listening to Your Life by Frederick Buechner
Simple Little Words: What You Say Can Change a Life by Michelle Cox and John Perrodin
Wounded by Words: Healing the Invisible Scars of Emotional Abuse by Susan Titus Osborn, Karen Kosman, and Jeenie Gordon
Chicken Soup for the Soul: Inspiring Stories of Hope, Devotion, Faith, and Miracles by Canfield, Hansen and Newman

Batter my heart, three-personed God; for You
As yet but knock, breathe, shine, and seek to mend;
That I may rise and stand, o'erthrow me, and bend
Your force to break, blow, burn, and make me new.

—John Donne, Holy Sonnet XIV[1]

CHAPTER FIVE

Spiritual Strategy #2:
Take Care of Yourself

R IGHT NOW, I have a pain in my neck, an unhappy reminder of a day years ago when I slipped and fell off a dock while trying to secure our boat. I fell between the dock and the boat, and the fall ruptured discs in my neck and dislocated and fractured my shoulder. After two surgeries and a lot of physical therapy, I got back to "normal," although my neck and shoulder will never be the same, and I must respect my old wound.

The physical pain is telling me that I have been sitting too long in front of the computer, that I need to take a break and go for a walk. The question is, Will I pay attention? And yes, I intend to go out for a walk . . . soon!

How do you feel right now? Listen to your body. Maybe you have an old wound—physical or emotional—that is asking for your attention.

Elijah's Story

Elijah was a mighty, fearless prophet who lived in Israel about 800 B.C. in the time of King Ahab and Queen Jezebel. The wickedness and idolatry under their control grew worse, and it was clear that

God's people, whom He had led out of Egypt, had forsaken Him. What would it take to get the people to listen? The prophet Elijah finally proclaimed a drought on the land: "As the LORD, the God of Israel, lives, whom I serve, there will be neither dew nor rain in the next few years except at my word" (1 Kings 17:1 NIV).

Three years into the drought, Elijah had a major showdown with the prophets of Baal. He called for the people to come to Mount Carmel, where he and the prophets of Baal had a contest to see who was the true God—Baal or the Lord. Elijah asked the people, "How long will you waver between two opinions?" (1 Kings 18:21 NIV). First, the prophets of Baal tried in vain to get their god to consume their sacrifice. Then it was Elijah's turn. Elijah called the people to come near. He repaired the altar of the Lord and then called down the fire of God. And God showed up—consuming the sacrifice in a mighty blaze, even though it was drenched with water. The people were convinced and declared, "The LORD, He *is* God!" (1 Kings 18:39). It was an amazing victory as Elijah had nearly nine hundred prophets of Baal destroyed.

Then the drought ended. You'd think after all of that, Elijah would take a deep breath and savor the victory. But when he heard Queen Jezebel say that she was going to kill him, he felt a pressing need to get out of town. Fast. So he ran alone into the wilderness. Exhausted, he fell asleep under a juniper tree. While he slept, an angel came and awakened him, and there was a cake baked on coals and a jar of water. The angel said, "Arise, and eat." He ate and drank, and again lay down to sleep. After he'd slept awhile, the angel of the LORD came again and touched him, and said, "Arise *and* eat, because the journey *is* too great for you" (1 Kings 19:5–8). So again, he ate and drank, and then went on his journey for forty days and nights to Mount Horeb.

When he got there, he went into a cave and spent the night. There, God spoke to him in a still, small voice: "What are you doing here, Elijah?" (1 Kings 19:12, 13).

Elijah had been through a lot: near starvation, the stress of watching people he loved abandon God, confronting King Ahab with the truth, and hiding in remote places for fear of being killed. Then there was the tremendous victory at Mount Carmel with the prophets of Baal. His physical body was worn out with all he'd been through and, even though Elijah was rugged and physically strong, the highs and lows had depleted him.

When Elijah was at his lowest while in the desert, he was finally ready to listen. And God asked him, "What are you doing here, Elijah?" (1 Kings 19:9). That's what He asks us, too, when we're finally ready to listen. Sometimes we can't hear Him until we've exhausted all our own effort, and then we finally hear Him asking, "What are you doing here, dear one?" Perhaps then, we can say with Christina Rossetti: "Speak, Lord, for Your servant hears. Grant me ears to hear, eyes to see, a will to obey, a heart to love; then declare what You will; reveal what You will; command what You will. Amen."[2]

> *Arise and eat, because the journey is too great for you.*
> —1 KINGS 19:7

The Mind-Body Connection

How would you care for a friend who had gone through extreme highs and lows or unbelievable stress? Perhaps he or she has suffered the loss of a loved one or a divorce or is going through bankruptcy. You would most likely urge him or her to get rest, to take a break.

Perhaps it's time to treat your own self as that friend. This can be hard for some of us who think we must care for everyone except ourselves. But caring for oneself is a matter of stewardship. If we aren't cared for, we cannot care for others.

Why do you not care for yourself? Maybe you don't believe you're worth it. Or that somehow you think you deserve the pain you're getting. "I failed, so I deserve to be punished."

> Perhaps it's time to treat your own self as that friend.

Life can take it out of you—changes, losses, disappointments. Grief can be exhausting. But there comes a time when the "drought" is over in our lives—after the loss, after the major stress, even after good things. And our physical bodies need to be replenished. "What's spiritual about that?" you may ask.

It is *very* spiritual. We are a package deal—body, soul, mind, and spirit. Our bodies instruct us. When we are worn out and pummeled by life, drawn into the desert, it is then that we can best hear His still, small voice speaking to us in that quiet place. As Psalm 51:6 reminds us, our "inward parts" really do "desire truth." We may feel lonely when claiming responsibility for ourselves, but it's the right thing to do. It is a healthy, empowering wise choice.

> Our bodies instruct us.

> *In the inward part You will make me to know wisdom.*
> —PSALM 51:6

The Importance of Physical Activity

There is overwhelming evidence of the benefits of physical exercise. According to Dr. Edward A. Taub, exercise can help prevent disease before it occurs. He also says, "Perhaps the most important benefit . . . is the effect it has on your psychological and spiritual outlook. Exercise makes your feelings of self-value and self-esteem soar. When you feel better about yourself, when you feel empowered and energetic, you make healthier choices in your eating and life-style habits."[3]

Brad and Susan, while going through their financial meltdown, realized they were depressed and filled with stress. Listening to the news every day only added to their anxiety. They couldn't seem to catch a break, even from the news. An AP-AOL study revealed that debt-related stress was 14 percent higher in 2008 than in 2004. Money is a leading source of stress for Americans; and today, more than three out of every four American families are in debt, according to the Federal Reserve's Survey of Consumer Finances. Those who report high levels of debt suffer stress from a range of stress-related illnesses, including ulcers, migraines, back pain, anxiety, depression, and heart attack.[4]

Brad and Susan needed to cut their budget, but both agreed they would keep their gym membership. Brad also stayed with his small Bible study group, an invaluable strength; and Susan picked up an old hobby, quilting, which she finds therapeutic.

I have found walking to be essential to my health. Besides helping keep my weight under control, I find it a great time to pray, to see the beauty of God's world, and to be reminded that God is in his heaven and all's right with the world.

Victor Parachin writes, "The truth is that a weakened body can lead to a weakened mind and spirit."[5] And according to James Blumenthal, professor of medical psychology at Duke University, "For some clinically depressed patients, exercise is as effective as the best medications we have."[6]

My friend Ruth, who lost her husband not long ago, always wanted to learn ballroom dancing. Although she's in her early seventies, she signed up for a class at the community college, and she is having a wonderful time.

> Making your health a priority is a choice, a decision that you make.

Karen, whose daughter was diagnosed with schizoaffective disorder, realized early on that she would not be able to help her own daughter if she was exhausted. At first, she got help with some medication to sleep, to break the cycle of sleeplessness. She gave herself permission to retreat for a while to restore herself. Karen now regularly takes walks outside and savors the beauty of nature, which she finds soothing and uplifting. She is committed to exercising at least five times a week and eats as nutritiously as possible. Dr. Edmund Jacobson said that "an anxious mind cannot exist in a relaxed body."[7]

Making your health a priority is a choice, a decision that you make, and it is a good choice. Richard Rohr writes, "We do not think ourselves into new ways of living. We live ourselves into new ways of thinking."[8]

We *choose* to do the right thing for ourselves. We acknowledge that, yes, we are getting a wake-up call from our body, and we determine that we are not going to hit the "snooze" button and ignore the warning signs; instead, we will tend to the care of ourselves.

Someone once said that we are like a house with four rooms, and to be balanced, we must go into all of those rooms each day. The "four rooms" could be described as your heart (that which you cherish), your soul (your emotions), your mind (your intellect), and your body (your physical being). Hans Selye, a pioneer in problems of stress, wrote, "The human body—like the tires on a car, or the rug on a floor—wears longest when it wears evenly. We can do ourselves a great deal of good . . . by just yielding to our natural cravings for variety in everyday life. We must not forget that the more we vary our actions, the less any one part suffers from attrition."[9]

What drove Elijah? For several years, he was driven by the huge challenge of getting his nation to turn around, to get right with God. Then, after the drought was over and after his amazing victory at Mount Carmel, he was driven into the wilderness by fear of Jezebel. Our lives have cycles: up, down. And the higher one cycle is, the lower the other one will be. We run on adrenaline, and then we are depleted. We need rest.

Thomas à Kempis wrote many centuries ago: "So long as you wear this mortal body, you will be subject to weariness and sadness of heart. . . . When this happens, you will be wise to resort to humble, exterior tasks to restore you by good works."[10]

The race is not to the swift,
Nor the battle to the strong,
Nor bread to the wise,
Nor riches to men of understanding,
Nor favor to men of skill;
But time and chance happen to all.
—ECCLESIASTES 9:11

The Importance of Rest

Are you sleeping well? Sleep restores us: "He makes me to lie down in green pastures. . . . He restores my soul" (Psalm 23:2–3). When we go through hard times, sleep is often one of the first things to go. Yet we need rest, to pace ourselves for the journey.

A lot of the early American pioneers going west on their epic journeys observed the Sabbath, a day of rest. Of course, there were some wagon trains that didn't, as they believed they needed to hurry to get over the mountains before the cold weather began. But those who did vote to keep the Sabbath knew they needed it for the journey, needed it to pace themselves. Their animals and children needed it as well.

> "I write in order to remember who I am."

Sometimes we think we don't have time to stop and rest, and yet what wisdom there is in it. In a journal entry, an early pioneer woman wrote that she felt overwhelmed by the land. She said, "I write in order to remember who I am."[11]

"There remains therefore a rest for the people of God" (Hebrews 4:9). In the thought-provoking and convicting book of Hebrews—especially chapters three and four—we are urged to make every effort to enter into rest, into belief. Why did God rest on the seventh day? Because His work was finished, and He stopped to savor the fact that it was done: "God saw that it was good" (Genesis 1:9).

Holidays and anniversaries help remind us of the real thing, of important commitments we've made. Birthdays help us celebrate the person, commemorate a milestone. And so it is with the "Sabbath" concept—it is an observance of the heart. Keeping the Sabbath helps us remember "that it is good." We can rest in His grace and provision for our lives and accept the work He has done.

Sometimes we must stop in order to go forward. We have lost the concept of Sabbath in our 24/7 world, but God created the Sabbath as a space of time to rest, to find our "center" in God again. Life can overwhelm us. When we take time to rest, to be still and find a place of quiet reflection, we "remember who we are."

When my husband and I were publishing magazines, we hired a consultant to help us redesign the magazine. After going over several issues, the consultant told us, "You have good articles as well as great graphics. But you have so much text and so many illustrations that it's confusing to the reader. You need more white space to set off the content of the articles. The magazine will be more readable."

His words reminded me of my life. I had a lot of good things in my life. But, it was too much. I needed "white space"—time to relax and breathe. Four years previously, I had been diagnosed with systemic lupus, but the medication did not seem to help and I was struggling. I finally went to the Mayo Clinic for a thorough examination. After several days of tests, I sat in Dr. O'Duffy's office. A short, wiry, Irish man with a mop of curly graying hair, he shot through me with his blue eyes. "I find no lupus. I believe you are neurologically and organically healthy. It is my belief that stress is the cause of your pain."

I said, "You mean it's *just stress?*"

He answered, "There's no such thing as *just* stress! Stress causes or exacerbates most major illnesses. Your mind, body, soul are interconnected, a package deal." He looked at my chart, which described my life—five children, magazine deadlines, too many commitments.

> "There's no such thing as *just* stress! Stress causes or exacerbates most major illnesses."

"Why do you have to do so much?" He told me, "You can continue to take all these medications you're on, or you can do something that is harder, but better. You can go home and confront your life and see why you have so much stress that you are in this much pain."

That was a short, but life-changing conversation for me. I went home, determined to listen to what God was telling me through my pain. I studied Dr. Hans Selye's book on stress and discovered that not all stress is bad. We need a certain amount to keep us on our toes, to meet deadlines. But as Dr. Selye explains, it is a matter of economics.[12]

Life is expendable. We spend it, so we must make deposits as well as withdrawals. If we don't, we will run in the red—like our bank account. I obviously was "in the red" emotionally and physically, and I did not know how to make deposits. This was a new language for me, but I went home determined to learn it. That wisdom changed my life.

> It is *vain for you to rise up early,*
> *To sit up late.*
> *To eat the bread of sorrows;*
> For so *He gives his beloved sleep.*
> —PSALM 127:2

The Importance of Nourishment

Nourish Your Body

There is a lot of good advice available on the Internet, as well as in books, regarding nutrition. If you feel you need professional guidance, you may want to schedule a consultation with a nutritionist. It's important to realize that when you're in stress mode, you experience surges of the hormone cortisol and sugar levels that spike and plummet, which can leave you feeling under pressure and sluggish. According to Elizabeth Somer, R.D., author of *The Food & Mood Cookbook*, we can counteract those reactions with the right foods.[13] For instance, for breakfast, avoid sugary cereals or breakfast bars and eat whole-grain cereal and a piece of fruit. Take a vitamin with at least 500 mg of calcium and 250 mg of magnesium.

Magnesium, which is flushed out when stress rushes in, helps regulate those cortisol levels. For a snack, veggie sticks help release a clenched jaw and the tension headache that results from stress.[14]

It is tempting when going through difficult times to "eat our stress." We can be tempted to overeat or choose high-fat and high-sugar food—"comfort food." A better, balanced approach is to try your best to choose foods closest to their natural state (fresh fruits, vegetables, salads, lean protein, and whole grains). Dr. Edward Taub advises choosing foods that naturally promote health, energy, and weight loss, and to see food not as the *enemy* but as your *energy*. His advice: "Everything in moderation, including moderation."[15]

Tone down the coffee by occasionally having green tea. Too much coffee with caffeine can raise levels of cortisol. Chamomile tea can help calm the mind and reduce stress, as can black tea. A study from the University College of London reported that participants who drank regular black tea displayed lower levels of cortisol and reported feeling calmer during six weeks of stressful situations than those who drank a placebo with the same amount of caffeine.[16]

> They said, "Can God prepare a table in the wilderness?"
> —PSALM 78:19

Nourish Your Soul

How can you nourish your soul? Take the time to relax, to take deep breaths. Take time to appreciate beauty. Take time to consider "the birds of the air" and "the lilies of the field" (Matthew 6:26, 28) and try to take in the thought of God's care for you.

You can also nourish your soul by expressing your creativity, and different people have different ways of doing that. Some people find that music feeds their soul; some love walking through an art gallery or savoring a few lines of good poetry. My husband enjoys working with his hands in his woodshop, creating amazing gifts. My soul is nourished by sitting at the piano, playing some Chopin or Debussy, or by listening to good music.

Perhaps making a craft or pursuing a hobby can nourish your soul. Somehow I don't think Elijah was the type of person who had a hobby, but it may have helped him be more balanced! Perhaps he'd enjoy birding, as Elijah was fed by ravens at one point in his life when they carried bread and meat to him!

Ask yourself, "What activity restores me? What am I doing when I lose complete track of time?" That could be a clue as to what activities restore your soul.

Paul Tournier wrote about the creative power within suffering: "If anything is certain, it is that every one of life's trials . . . creates, like the plowing of a field, an empty space where seed can be sown. In the sudden void caused by a bereavement . . . an illness . . . failure . . . loneliness . . . your mind is assailed by fundamental questions to which you hardly ever gave a thought in the coercive whirl of life."[17]

> "No man ever sank under the burden of the day. It is when tomorrow's burden is added to the burden of today that the weight is more than a man can bear."

O God, you are my God; I earnestly search for you.
My soul thirsts for you;
my whole body longs for you in this parched and weary land
where there is no water.
—Psalm 63:1 NLT

Nourish Your Mind

Angela Tucker, mom of Samuel, the baby born with many special needs, is also a busy pastor's wife and has two other active children with busy sports schedules. Angela told me, "I have learned to put Samuel's condition in a little box up on a shelf and not take it down unless I have to. I don't think about the diagnosis or the prognosis any more than I have to. I just look at him as Samuel, my son."

George MacDonald wrote words of wisdom: "No man ever sank under the burden of the day. It is when tomorrow's burden is added to the burden of today that the weight is more than a man can bear. Never load yourself so. If you find yourself so loaded, at least remember this: it is your doing, not God's. He begs you to leave the future to him, and mind the present."[18]

What are your "rehearsed speeches"—you know, the tapes that play in your head? Elijah had a rehearsed speech: "I have been very zealous for the LORD God of hosts; because the children of Israel have forsaken Your covenant, torn down Your altars, and killed Your prophets with the sword. I alone am left; and they seek to take my life" (1 Kings 19:10, 14).

Elijah had a lot of time in the wilderness to go over that speech. He recited the exact same speech to both the angel God sent him and to God Himself. Our self-talk is important. It shapes how we feel; it shapes how we live. *If only I had intervened in Amy's situation. Maybe if she'd been living at home, this wouldn't have happened.* Or, *Where did I screw up as a mother?* Others may think, *If I had been a better husband, we wouldn't have gone through a divorce.* Or, *If I'd managed our finances better, we wouldn't be in that situation.* If . . . if . . . if! And on and on, ad infinitum.

Self-talk is powerful, and often we are not even aware of why we are saying what we do to ourselves. Sometimes we are agreeing with negative voices of the past, and those voices are powerful.

My friend Kathy grew up with an older brother who constantly called her names. She's now fifty, and she told me she had an epiphany when she realized her internal dialogue was agreeing with what her brother called her as a child: "Fat pig." Then she'd go eat something not good for her, living up to *his* definition of her, not her own—and certainly not God's. We can nourish our minds by understanding that each of us is a wonderful, unique creation, and we can agree with God's definition of us.

This means taking time to read the Bible, to adopt a reading plan and stick with it, just as we adopt a healthy food plan. Reading scripture nourishes our minds and souls and gives us faith to go on and the hope that things are going to get better.

To discover what you truly believe about yourself, examine your self-talk. What are you *feeling* about yourself? You may know what you *should* believe, but you still feel negatively toward yourself. Why do you think you feel that way? Does it agree with God's opinion of you?

> To discover what you truly believe about yourself, examine your self-talk.

We can also choose to nourish our minds by reading faith-filled, hope-filled books and by not being consumed with the bad news that is so readily available. Nourishing our minds also means considering the movies we watch, our television habits, the sites we visit on the Internet. When we go through tough times, our minds are vulnerable, and we can take the responsibility to feed our minds faith—not fear.

God will speak wisdom to us in our desert experiences and remind us that He is God. Elijah carried the whole weight of the kingdom on his shoulders. His "rehearsed speech" showed his mind-set: "I have been very zealous for the Lord. . . . I alone am left." But the truth of the matter was, he wasn't alone, even though he had convinced himself that he was. There was another righteous man, Obadiah, who worked for the king and risked Jezebel's wrath to hide one hundred prophets in a cave during the drought, secretly bringing them food and water. Evidently Elijah was oblivious to Obadiah's heroics and to the faith of the one hundred prophets he'd hidden. God had to remind Elijah that there were seven thousand people who had not bowed to Baal.

Stress is not "out there"; it's *inside us*. It's important to pay attention to our feelings, to realize what we're going through. But the key to success in the wilderness is to pay attention to what God is saying to us through our pain, to trust Him there.

> *Do not worry about your life. . . .*
> *Look at the birds of the air;*

they do not sow or reap or store away in barns,
and yet your heavenly Father feeds them.
Are you not much more valuable than they?
—MATTHEW 6:25–26

You Live What You Believe

What we believe affects how we live. Susanna Wesley, mother of John and Charles Wesley, said, "There are two things to do about the Gospel—believe it and behave it."[19] What we live becomes our theology.

When I became sick and had to go to the Mayo Clinic, my problem was more than physical. It was theological—I was living what I believed: I believed that I had to work to prove that I was acceptable, and that belief worked its way into my physical body. I learned a fresh appreciation for the grace of God: "By grace you have been saved . . . not of ourselves, lest any man should boast" (Ephesians 2:8, 9).

You *can* change what you believe and, therefore, how you live. One of the first things you can do is *believe that you can change.* Stop saying you can't. Instead, repeat to yourself, "I can do all things through Christ, who strengthens me" (Philippians 4:13). Our change comes through Christ—through faith in the power of His resurrection—not through the power of positive thinking or anything we can generate on our own.

The second thing you can do is *clarify what you need from God.* Jesus asked of the blind man who was crying out for mercy, "What do you want ME to do for you?" (Luke 18:41). Jesus obviously knew that the man was blind, but He asked the man to articulate what he needed from God. The power goes where the focus is. We can tell God what we need from Him.

When I got my wake-up call from Dr. O'Duffy, I realized I would not think of treating my friends the way I was driving myself. Like Elijah, we can be driven into side trips that God never intended for us to take; and depleted, we run on empty. Jesus called us His friends, an amazing thought. Just as we would encourage our friends to restore themselves, Jesus calls us to restoration—body, soul, mind, and spirit. Stewardship is the conscientious management of things that matter. And you matter.

The week before Amy's baby was born, I had a dream. I was doing a gardening project—I had lots of weeds and flowers that needed tending. In my dream, I saw a dark-haired little girl with her mother, a woman with longer dark hair and a round face. She had an anxious, troubled look in her eyes. I took the little girl's hand. "Is it all right if she comes with me and helps me?" I wanted her very much to be with me. The mother said reluctantly, "Well, I guess that's all right. Just bring her back when you're through."

"Oh, I will," I said, and the little girl and I went off together and began working in the soil, as if it was the most natural thing in the world to do. Good, satisfying, and creative work. I thought, "This little girl really is mine. But later I will make sure she gets back to that other woman."

I awoke, wondering what that meant. As I've thought about it, I think the dark-haired woman is Amy's birth mother and the little girl is Amy. I knew it was important to return to Korea with Amy, and the dream helped convince me to make the trip a priority. Our trip has been an important part of Amy's healing.

When Amy was in high school, she had nightmares about her birth mother leaving her. Although she has no concrete memories of her birth mother and was left at a baby home when she was only three months old, Amy dreamed often of seeing a dark-haired woman walk away from her. Amy said she could never see her face. She would awaken, arms outstretched, with tears of grief and rage running down her face.

It is a helpless feeling as a mother not to be able to kiss away such deep hurts. But I don't believe our story is finished yet. There are some complex, life-defining wounds that take time and years to heal. A friend copied out this verse and gave it to me the morning Amy relinquished her baby:

The LORD will guide you continually
And satisfy your soul in drought
And strengthen your bones;
You shall be like a well-watered garden,
And like a spring of water, whose waters do not fail.
—ISAIAH 58:11

PERSONAL REFLECTION

Read Elijah's story in 1 Kings 19. How does his restoration in the wilderness speak to you?

1. Do you experience chronic physical pain? What "message" do you think your body is sending you?

2. Is there an emotional pain that you are carrying? Describe it.

3. Consider asking for prayer for healing, and remember that He said, "I am the God that heals you." Write your prayer in your journal.

4. Which of the four areas of your life (body, mind, soul, and spirit) most need restoration? Why?

5. Write out some actual, practical goals to help restore you.

NEW BEGINNINGS RESOURCE

Helping You Reach Out

Many hospitals have foundations that offer wonderful, targeted programs to help you achieve your wellness goals. Take advantage of what is available in your community.

Get out of your "rut"—consider pursuing a hobby you've always wanted to take up, or explore new interests.

Recommended reading:

You: The Owner's Manual by Drs. Michael Roizen and Mehmet Oz

In His Image by Dr. Paul Brand and Philip Yancey

20 Things Adoptive Parents Need to Succeed by Sherrie Eldredge (Encourages self-care for adoptive parents)

Defeating Depression: Real Hope for Life-Changing Wholeness, by Leslie Vernick

Come Closer: A Call to Life, Love, and Breakfast on the Beach, by Jane Rubietta

O God our Father, we are learning the hard way,

the way of experience,

that to reap fellowship we must give fellowship.

Help us then to give fellowship open-handedly,

not because we want to reap it, but because we can't help it.

Amen.

—E. Stanley Jones[1]

CHAPTER SIX

Spiritual Strategy #3:
Reach Out to Other People

A FEW MONTHS AFTER my father died, my mother was alone on Sunday for the first time. She stopped to eat at a restaurant, but as she sat at her table for one, the impact of being alone hit her. Mother couldn't eat and fled the restaurant in tears. She told me later, "Eating is a fellowship."

It is true. We are nourished and sustained not only by good food but also by being with one another, sharing our lives in good times as well as bad times.

There are two movements in a relationship: giving and receiving. We give gifts; we receive gifts. We give help; we receive help. We give prayer; we receive prayer.

My Welsh grandmother used to say, "There are two types of people: givers and takers." I didn't fully know what she meant, but I certainly didn't want to be a taker. I wanted to be a giver. Brad and Susan, the California couple who went through bankruptcy, had always been givers. It was a humbling moment for Brad to receive a check from his son, as he and Susan found themselves in a place where they had to receive in order to survive. Susan said, "It's been a blow to my pride to have to accept help from our children."

We Need People

You may be like Brad and Susan and find it easier to give than to receive. I, too, have a difficult time accepting help. But what we often fail to understand is that when we learn to receive, we are giving. We bless others by receiving, and it takes humility and grace to do so. Thomas Merton observed this about the paradox of giving and receiving love: "The gift of love is the gift of the power and the capacity to love, and therefore, to give love with full effect is also to receive it. So love can only be kept by being given away, and it can only be given perfectly when it is also received."[2]

> When we learn to receive, we are giving. We bless others by receiving.

Some people are wired to be more relational, and it's natural for them to reach out, to get into others' lives. Some of us are more private people, and it may be the scariest thing in the world to pick up a phone to call someone or to walk into a support group. Regardless, it takes risk and effort to reach out. It takes honesty and vulnerability.

We can ask a friend, "How are you?" not really wanting to know. Or when asked, we reply with a smile, "I'm fine, thanks," when inside we are dying. We hold back and deny one another true fellowship. But our need for authentic relationship is put in us by God, who created us in his image. Relationship takes giving and receiving.

Surely the unique pain of divorce is of love not received or of love that is rejected. It can be so personal, as Jim McClelland discovered. Our life stories are filled with themes of giving and receiving love, as well as loss and rejection. For most of us, all of those ingredients are mixed together. This is life.

When we experience abandonment or loss or rejection, we can be tempted to withdraw from others for fear of more rejection. Why keep trying? What if our reaching out is not received or is misunderstood? What if we lose again?

The only way out of that cycle is to reach out, no matter what. That's what the Bible itself is all about—God's pursuit of us and our reaching out for Him.

Rejoice with those who rejoice,
and weep with those who weep.
—ROMANS 12:15

Naomi and Ruth's Story

Naomi and Ruth's story is a story of giving and receiving grace.

When Naomi came back home to Bethlehem after the loss of her husband and two sons, people hardly recognized her: "Can this be Naomi?"

"No," she said. "Do not call me Naomi; call me Mara, for the Almighty has dealt very bitterly with me. I went out full, and the LORD has brought me home again empty" (Ruth 1:20, 21). Naomi grieved hard. She was mad at God: "The Almighty did this to me!"

Family stories throughout time tell the common epic of love and loss. Life's storms overtake them: wars, famine, and addictions. Illness, divorce, and death can decimate families. That's why we are captivated by books and novels and movies about family dramas—they can be riveting. When we gather during the holidays and talk to our parents, our grandparents, and aunts and uncles, we need to hear our family's stories. We may have to do some digging to get the whole story, but there's a lot of drama in our stories—some more than in others!

But beyond the drama, there's the rest of the story—how people are restored, put back together, and go on with new life and hope. What makes the difference between those who thrive and those who continue in their pain? I believe that those who keep reaching out and keep putting themselves in places to get help are the ones who finally find new hope. And then they are able to give back what they receive.

> What makes the difference between those who thrive and those who continue in their pain?

And so it was with Naomi's story, which became Ruth's story, too. Naomi didn't return to Bethlehem alone—Kilion's young widow, Ruth, came with her. Naomi and Elimelech and their two sons, Mahlon and Kilion, had started out years before in Bethlehem with high hopes. When famine hit, they went to Moab where there was opportunity. Things didn't go so well for them. First, Elimelech died. By this time their sons had grown, and Naomi arranged to have her sons married to Orpah and Ruth, local women. And then both of her sons died, too, not leaving any children. Naomi's losses were piling up: first, Naomi had moved far away from her home and family; then her husband died; and then *both* of her sons, with no grandchildren. In those days, the extinction of the family line was unthinkable, and Naomi was facing that loss. She could identify with the psalmist: "I am distraught. . . . Loved one and friend You have put far from me, *and* my acquaintances into darkness" (Psalm 88:15, 18).

Even though Naomi felt abandoned and empty, she acknowledged her helplessness and need, and she reached out. We can learn a lot from Naomi.

Naomi Reached Out for Good News

After all the bad news of the loss in her life, when Naomi heard that the famine at home was over, she decided to do something. It may have taken her a while, but she made concrete plans to return to Bethlehem.

Even when we're in pain, we can look for good news, for something positive. Scripture verses of hope and restoration and healing can be powerful, and we can feed on them. Brad and Susan kept looking for the silver lining for their financial disaster. After they talked to their bank and their mortgage company, they did find a glimmer of hope. It may take real effort and courage to try to see anything positive, but when we do, we can move toward it.

Naomi Put Herself in a Place Where Healing Was Possible

Naomi made a constructive choice to move to be near extended family. Naomi didn't wait until she "felt" whole, she took actual steps to go back to Bethlehem.

We can put ourselves in places where healing can begin: a positive church environment or a small study group, or we can join a support system. We can intentionally strengthen ties with positive, nourishing people. For myself, I have found it healing and life-affirming to help students with their music at a local elementary school. It is wonderful to see the lights go on in their eyes as they develop their talents and create something beautiful.

> We can intentionally strengthen ties with positive, nourishing people.

Naomi Reached Out to Orpah and Ruth

In the midst of Naomi's grief, she saw there were other people hurting, too. She realized that her daughters-in-law were young—there was still time for them to remarry, have children. On the way back to Bethlehem, she told them, "Go back to your mother's house." In essence, she said, "I can't supply you with another husband. Get on with your life." Orpah finally agreed and kissed Naomi good-bye.

The Bible doesn't tell us the rest of Orpah's story. We wonder—whatever became of her? Did she find happiness? It must have been painful for Naomi to watch the retreating figure of her daughter-in-law—Mahlon's young widow—go back to her people, her gods. Another relationship lost. There are unfinished stories in all our lives, stories that are left hanging. We love the best we can, we reach out the best we can, and sometimes our love is rejected or ignored. Nonetheless, Naomi reached out to Orpah, seeking her daughter-in-law's best interest.

But then there was Ruth, who clung to Naomi and spoke those wonderful words of commitment that we cherish: "Entreat me not to leave you, *or to* turn back from following after you; For wherever you go, I will go; And wherever you lodge, I will lodge; Your people shall be my people, And your God, my God" (Ruth 1:16).

I wonder if Naomi fully appreciated Ruth's commitment to her at that time. Perhaps not, as she was still consumed by grief. Yet over time, something wonderful would happen for Naomi, and her life would be restored in surprising ways.

In our loss, we can reach out by remembering that others within our circle may be hurting, too. A loss or crisis affects everyone in the family. It was only after the relinquishment of Amy's baby that I pulled out of my own sorrow to see the birth father, Jeff. He had steadfastly supported Amy every step of the way and agreed with her that they needed to do the hardest thing ever: give their baby to parents who were ready to be parents. He needed comfort and support, too. I will be forever grateful to him for his unselfish love. And I needed to see the grief my own husband was experiencing, as well as that of all of our children, who keenly felt the loss—not only for Amy and Jeff but also for themselves. I was also surprised at the feelings of loss from our extended family as well—cousins, aunts, and uncles. Even in our deepest pain, we must take time to lift our eyes and see the pain of others.

> The natural rhythms of life help to heal us; they carry us forward as we keep reaching out.

Naomi Invested in Ruth

As Naomi began caring for someone besides herself, she became interested in life again. She invested herself in Ruth by advising her on how to pursue Boaz—the man who eventually became Ruth's husband. Naomi began to forge new relationships and loyalties, and she renewed old ones. Harvest was on, and she got caught up in the season.

The natural rhythms of life help to heal us; they carry us forward as we keep reaching out. The law of the harvest is an undeniable principle. We invest time and love in those God puts in our lives, and over time, what we put out will return somehow. Loving others doesn't demand "warm and fuzzy" thoughts. We may not feel warm or fuzzy. Love can be simply considering what we can do to make life better for someone and then doing it. To truly love someone is to try to understand what would be good for him or her and facilitate that to the best of our ability. Love never fails. It is true, some seeds of love don't take root. The ground can be hard or it's crowded with weeds. Orpah chose not to stay with Naomi. But Ruth did. The results are God's business; ours is to *reach out*, regardless. Keep investing in people, no matter what. There will be a return someday, in God's economy.

Fulfillment Was Restored to Naomi

As time and seasons passed, Naomi found new life. Ruth and Boaz got married and had a baby boy they named Obed. Naomi became their nanny, and once again, Naomi's arms were full. It's interesting to note that the name *Obed* is a Hebrew word that means "God's servant."[3] It is often through serving that we receive fulfillment and healing.

When Naomi's grandson was born, the neighboring women affirmed her: "Blessed *be* the LORD, who has not left you this day without a close relative. . . . May he be to you a restorer of life and a nourisher of your old age; for your daughter-in-law, who loves you, who is better to you than seven sons, has born him" (Ruth 4:14, 15).

"I will restore health to you and heal you of your wounds,"
says the LORD.
Thus says the LORD, "Yes, I have loved you
with an everlasting love;
Therefore with loving kindness I have drawn you.
Again I will build you, and you shall be rebuilt."
—JEREMIAH 30:17; 31:3

Christie and David's Story

Relationships are everything. That is why it is so hard to lose someone, especially a child.

Christie and David suffered an unimaginable tragedy on August 28, 2002. Prior to this date, they had two beautiful children, Skyler, their three-year-old daughter, and Tyler, their nine-month-old son. After this date, they had only one. Christie says, "I look at the picture of my three-year-old Skyler and wonder what she would look like now, at nine years of age? Sometimes that day seems like yesterday; sometimes it seems forever ago."

David was home; Tyler, their nine-month-old, was sleeping. Christie was going to run a few errands, and David came to unlock the back gate so Christie could back the car out of the garage. She said, "I watched Skyler disappear into the house. Then I started to back out. I thought I hit the house and thought, *How did I do that?*

"And then I screamed. I knew right away. David came and pulled her out. I fell to my knees, screaming. My neighbors said later it was the most primal scream they'd ever heard. David said, 'Call 9-1-1.' Later, I remembered saying to the 9-1-1 operator, '*I think I just killed my baby.*'"

David handed Skyler's limp body to Christie. Christie says that Skyler was unrecognizable, as the tire had gone over her head. Christie sat on the grass and held her. When the paramedics got there, Christie kept telling them Skyler was trying to breathe. She wasn't. It was her final moments.

Christie says, "It was trauma. Complete trauma. That night we were supposed to have dinner at David's parents. He called his parents and said, 'Go find our pastor. Dinner tonight is off. Skyler is dead.'"

"Go find our pastor. Dinner tonight is off. Skyler is dead."

Their pastor came. Christie says, "He blessed Skyler the day she came and the day she left. He was here every single day for months."

While Christie and David's story is every parent's nightmare, what is remarkable about their story is how they were surrounded by people who wouldn't let them go through their tragedy alone—and Christie and David reached out to them, receiving their help. From the very first, their pastor was with them all the way. At Skyler's memorial service, their pastor told their church, "David and Christie have a cross to bear. And it's also our cross to bear."

David and Christie also reached out to each other. Two days after the accident, David came to Christie with tears streaming down his face. He said, "My very first thought was, *My daughter's dead.* And the next thought was, *Am I going to lose my wife?* Seventy-five percent of parents who lose their children divorce." David said to Christie, "I refuse to be part of that statistic!"

Christie says, "Six years later, I can tell you I have seen so many blessings. Yes, it was a complete tragedy. For months, I wanted to die. I said, *'Just take me home, God.'* I was in denial at first. I would go into Skyler's room, feel the cover on her bed. I experienced just God-awful, raw pain." Our pastor said, "God's a big guy. He can handle your pain, your rage. When you're angry at God, you're probably closer to Him than at any other time."

David and Christie reached out to a grief counselor and also joined a support group, Compassionate Friends, a group for parents who suffer the loss of a child. They needed to be with others who knew their pain.

Christie says, "I didn't drive for a long time. Once when I was driving, I saw a huge vehicle, and I thought, *How easy it would be just to drive into that truck and just end it all.*" But an unlikely person emerged to help Christie.

Christie's grandparents had lost their daughter years before, but her grandfather had never talked about his own loss. But after Skyler's death, he began to call Christie every day. Christie saw her own grandparents find healing from the loss of their daughter years before, as they reached out to their granddaughter in her loss. Christie and her grandfather ended up with an incredibly close bond.

Christie's mother reached out to Christie, too. She shared that when, as a child, her sister died, her parents had pushed her and her sisters away in their grief. She warned Christie, "Don't do to your son what my parents did to me and my sisters." Christie saw how easily that could happen; as she would hold Tyler, her heart was guarded. Christie remembers, "I was scared to get close to Tyler." One day she watched Tyler pull himself up. She remembers thinking, "I know this baby needs me, and I need him." At that very moment, her little guy laid his head down on her knee, and Christie scooped him up and said, "Mommy just remembered how much I need you!"

Healing has been a process for David and Christie. She said, "I didn't know how I could forgive myself. I was at a loss, but I dove into my Bible and looked up in the concordance everything about forgiveness. It taught me that God forgives us for *everything*. And I have to keep going there. I know it was an accident.

"People told me, 'Time heals.' And I wanted to tell them, 'Blow it out your ear!' The first year was excruciating. The second year was hard. The third year, I thought it would kill me. But this year, six years out, I feel at peace."

> "People told me, 'Time heals.' And I wanted to tell them, 'Blow it out your ear!'"

Three years ago, David and Christie were blessed by the birth of another daughter, Grace Nicole. Christie says she looks a lot like Skyler.

Christie now reaches out to other parents who have suffered the traumatic loss of a child, and she sends notes or cards. One father, who accidentally ran over his eighteen-month-old son, told her, "I received hundreds of sympathy notes—but yours was different. You know the hole of pain I am in."

Eventually David and Christie left their support group, Compassionate Friends. They realized there was a time to move on and live in the honor of their loved one, which they do. Christie says, "I focus on the blessings. I focus on life. This is not a short journey; it is a lifetime journey."

Christie and David experienced what it meant in the truest way to lean on their pastor, their family, and their friends. Now they reach out to comfort others, and their words of comfort and reassurance are powerful.

> *Praise be to the God and Father of our* LORD *Jesus Christ,*
> *the Father of compassion and the God of all comfort,*
> *who comforts us in all our troubles, so that we can comfort*
> *those in any trouble with the comfort we ourselves*
> *have received from God.*
> *For just as the sufferings of Christ flow over into our lives,*
> *so also through Christ our comfort overflows . . . our hope*
> *for you is firm,*
> *because we know that just as you share in our sufferings,*
> *so also you share in our comfort.*
> —2 CORINTHIANS 1:3–7

Your Story

Like Naomi, and Christie and David, you have a story, too. The details are different, but the pain is the same. Following are two simple helps that can be applied to *your* story. From Naomi and from David and Christie, we learn the value of *asking for help* and of *giving out of our experience.* You, too, my friend, can find new hope and life on the other side of your impossible year or years.

Ask for Help

What carries us through crisis and loss?

You know—it's the people who show up and carry you when you can scarcely carry yourself. It has been said that sorrow shared is sorrow diminished. Sometimes, we need to take the initiative and *ask* for that help.

There's something especially wonderful about *praying* friends. After Karen's daughter was finally diagnosed with schizoaffective disorder, a small group of women gathered to pray for her every Friday morning for a year. Karen is still overwhelmed by that generous act of love.

Jim McClelland's best friend showed up to help him pack and move on the day when Jim and his wife separated. Jim said, "It's important to surround yourself with people who can help you because some burdens are too heavy to bear alone. I had a few key people in my life, and I leaned on them."

When our family went through the dilemma of Amy's pregnancy, my sister Janie came and walked the river with me, and as we walked, we talked and cried. She didn't minimize our dilemma or try to give us immediate solutions. She listened and asked a few thoughtful questions.

I am also blessed to belong to a group of women who meet weekly to study the Bible and pray for one another. We have been through a lot together, and these women are like soul sisters. We trust each other. Someone said, "Friendship is the relationship we all need to help us through our other relationships."

One can never underestimate the simple power of presence, the simple power of being with one another on life's journey. Most people don't need instruction; we just need to be reminded of what we know. It has been said that a true friend is someone who, when you forget your song, comes and sings it for you.

> One can never underestimate the simple power of presence.

People can be amazingly wonderful when you go through a hard time. But then as time goes by, people get on with their lives. And that may be the time when you need to take responsibility for your healing and reach out for objective and professional counsel. During the divorce proceedings, Jim went to a mandated class on how to handle joint custody. He said, "I wasn't excited about going at first, but I was surprised to see how helpful the class was for both myself and my ex-wife as we concentrated on trying to help our sons the best we could in our situation."

There may be a time when you need to ask for prayer. It is humbling, but powerful to ask for help. James reminds us:

> *Confess your trespasses to one another,*
> *and pray for one another, that you may be healed.*
> —JAMES 5:16

Give out of Your Experience

Going through difficulty gives us wisdom we would not have otherwise. I was a young mom in my twenties when my father died. The day after, in the midst of relatives coming and planning the funeral, I came home to find a large pan of lasagna on the kitchen counter from my friend Denise. She had lost both her mother and father early in her life, and she knew just what to do and what to say. She scribbled on the back of a used envelope: *I love you so much, and I'm so sorry! I'm praying for your family. Put your hope in Jesus, because He never fails.*

> Going through difficulty gives us wisdom we would not have otherwise.

There was something so spontaneous and encouraging about that note scribbled on the back of an envelope. A young mom herself, she probably didn't have time to go out and buy a flowery card. But she took the time to make a supper for us and brought it over. Years later, I remember the comfort her kind action brought our family. *She knew.* That is what sorrow or difficulty will do—it can make us more compassionate givers and help us understand and love people. It gives us credibility to reach out to others in their pain.

Henri Nouwen wisely said, "Who can take away suffering without entering into it? The great illusion of leadership is to think that others can be led out of the desert by someone who has never been there."[4]

How can you give to others out of your pain? What specifically can you do? Here are two simple things:

You Can Listen

Can you think of someone in your life—perhaps when you were a child—who genuinely listened to you? Perhaps you are fortunate enough to have someone in your life now who listens to you. When you're with him or her, you feel most fully yourself; somehow you feel visible, more alive, just by being with this person. Listening is one of the most powerful ways to say to someone, "I care about you." We can give this wonderful gift to others, and the only cost to us is our time—and resisting the urge to interrupt or the right to be "right" all the time! James writes, "Let every man be swift to hear, slow to speak, slow to wrath" (James 1:19).

Who in your life needs you to listen? It takes a conscious effort to truly listen—to study the body language, to listen to what lies "between the lines," to hear beyond the obvious, to listen to the tone in a voice, or to notice an expression. It takes effort to listen more to what is *not* being said than to what is being said. What a gift we give someone by taking time to listen!

The Swiss psychiatrist Paul Tournier wrote, "I am convinced that nine out of every ten persons seeing a psychiatrist do not need one. They need somebody who will love them with God's love . . . and they will get well."[5]

You Can Give of Your Time

Take time for people. In the end, that's really all that matters—loving and caring for people. We can take time to stop and visit with someone in the store or at the post office or after church. A friend who'd recently lost her husband was surprised to see some people avoid talking to her, as if she were contagious. It doesn't take much to just take the time to say, "How are you?" and really mean it.

I love the practical spin James Bryan Smith puts on the value of giving of our time:

Life is too short to refuse to offer a kind word to someone who needs it, too short to turn a deaf ear to someone who is hurting, and too short to pass by someone who needs a hand. Life is too short to withhold a Word of life, too short not to pray for someone we know is in trouble, and too short to neglect that note of encouragement we were meaning to send.

Life is too short not to send toys to children with life-threatening diseases, too short not to offer to babysit for exhausted parents, and too short not to give your co-worker a bouquet of flowers. Life is too short not to shovel your neighbor's walk, too short not to visit a retirement home for an afternoon, and too short not to spend a morning writing letters to people we love. Life is too short to let a week pass without hearing someone say, "Thank you."[6]

Life's pressure is always there; everyone is busy. We all have our own stuff to deal with, and we can become isolated by our work and our schedules. The only way to solve that is to open up. To take time to reach out. Jesus said it simply: "Freely you have received, freely give" (Matthew 10:8).

It doesn't have to be much. A phone call, a note, stopping by with a bunch of flowers or a plate of cookies. Little things that say, "I'm here, and I care."

> *Bear one another's burdens,*
> *And so fulfill the law of Christ.*
> —GALATIANS 6:2

Reaching out can be a risk. What if, when we reach out, someone doesn't hear us or understand? What if, in our reaching out to others, we are ignored or rejected? Love is a risk. Life can be messy and inconvenient. Sometimes we get burned in a relationship.

But love is worth the risk. If you doubt that, remember the cross. Jesus spread out his arms to show us how much He loves us, and His love was and is rejected by many. Even though He knew He would be rejected, He still went to the cross, and He still is not willing that any should perish. Keep reaching out. Love is worth it.

Remember these simple thoughts: We can't fix people, *but we can love them*. We can't solve some situations, *but we can do the right thing within the situation*. We don't always understand God's ways, *but we can trust Him, anyway*.

There are some risks to loving. *And it's worth it.*

PERSONAL REFLECTION

Read the story of Ruth. How did she—over time—find healing by reaching out?

1. Do you find it easy to ask for the help you need?

2. Ask yourself, *If I am not reaching out to others, why not?*

3. List some ways of reaching out that you believe may help facilitate your healing.

4. What are ways to invest in someone you care about?

5. Think of two constructive ways you can give out of your experience . . . then do them!

NEW BEGINNINGS RESOURCE

Starting New Relationships

Do you need a friend? Real relationships don't just happen. It takes effort and commitment. Ask yourself the following questions:

- *Do I pursue a relationship, go out of my way if necessary?* In John 4, Jesus met the Samaritan woman at the well. He went out of His way to meet her.

- *Do I willingly give of myself?* In John 6, Jesus fed the multitude with a boy's simple lunch.

- *Do I risk vulnerability?* The writer of Ephesians says, "we should no longer be children, tossed to and fro and carried about . . . but speaking the truth in love, may grow up in all things into Him" (Ephesians 4:14,15).

You might consider reaching out to join a support group that is appropriate for your situation, such as:

- Compassionate Friends (an organization for parents who have lost a child)

- Grief recovery groups

- Small groups available through the church

- Volunteer!

Recommended Reading
11 Indispensable Relationships You Can't Be Without by Leonard Sweet

Face-to-Face with Naomi and Ruth: Together for the Journey by Janet Thompson

Why Can't I Make People Understand? by Lisa Copen (deals with chronic illness)

Reaching Out by Henri Nouwen

Our life is a warfare, our whole life.
It is not only with lusts
in our youth and ambitions in our middle years,
and in devotions in our age,
but with agonies in our body and tentations in our spirit
upon our death-bed that we are to fight.
And he cannot be said to overcome,
that fights not out the whole battle.

—John Donne, *Sermons*[1]

CHAPTER SEVEN

Spiritual Strategy #4: Put One Foot in Front of the Other

How do you grapple with life when you're tired of the battle, and you'd rather run away and hide or crawl in bed and stay there? But you know you can't. You know that somehow you must keep going. How do you put one foot in front of the other when your dreams have died?

A few months into Amy's pregnancy, I was participating in a life-coaching program, a program I had signed up for some time previously. The material was excellent. I knew it was good. I could tell. But as I looked at the sheet asking me to list strategic goals and vision for my future, my mind was numb. Goals? Vision? Strategic planning? *Yeah, right.* The only kind of goals I could even contemplate were of the simplest nature: How about getting a complete night's sleep? How about getting my blood pressure in the normal range? Maybe I could make a goal to take a walk and actually enjoy it. Or perhaps have lunch with a friend and not have her pity me because our family is in crisis. But there was no way I could consider the huge goals our presenter was suggesting.

When you're experiencing the first weeks, months, year, years, after a loss, your goal is simply to put one foot in front of the other, day after day. It's survival. It's being stubbornly determined to keep going, to do the right thing, regardless of how you feel. This is the soul-grinding process that changes us from a victim to a victor. It doesn't happen in one easy instant, and it is unglamorous and so very *daily*.

Perhaps you have a situation that is causing you great concern. You pray; you believe; you get help; you try to fix it. Then you or your loved one hits one of life's bumps, and there you are, back to square one again. Or maybe you've had a life-defining loss and you're trying to get through the "valley of the shadow," back to normal—whatever that is. But the valley seems *so long*. How do you get through when there seems to be no way?

> "I just want to get to a place where this doesn't define and consume my every waking moment."

Brad and Susan often felt as if they were slogging through wet cement, trying to solve their financial mess. One evening Brad said to Susan, "I just want to get to a place where this doesn't define and consume my every waking moment."

Have you ever felt like that? I certainly have.

In the Old Testament, we see another journey that required the sojourners to take one step at a time—slowly, diligently, daily. As the Israelites traveled from Egypt to the land God had promised them, they traversed a long and difficult road through a barren wilderness. Sometimes they rose to the challenge admirably; sometimes they failed miserably. Kind of like us. From them, we can learn eight steps we can take as we travel through our own wilderness.

1. Follow Your Leader (He Knows the Way!)

The Israelites had been in slavery in Egypt for generations, when God called Moses to lead them back to Canaan, their promised land. They needed a guide to take them through unfamiliar territory. And so do we.

Joan Chittister writes, "The great interruptions of life leave us completely disoriented. We become lost. The map of life changes overnight and our sense of direction and purpose goes with it. Life comes to a halt, takes on a new and indiscernible shape. Promise fails us, and it is the loss of promise that dries in our throats. What was is no more and what is to come, if anything, is unclear."[2]

What got the Israelites through the wilderness was following Moses, who was listening to God. When they finally left Egypt, they thought they were home free—until they got to the Red Sea and realized Pharaoh's army was behind them. Now what? They were trapped, with no good options. Pharaoh said of the children of Israel, "They *are* bewildered by the land, the wilderness has closed them in" (Exodus 14:3). He thought he had them.

The enemy of our soul may think he "has us," too—trapped, with no good options. We wonder, *What's this all about, God? I don't see how to get through.* But when we follow our Leader, we will see some amazing things happen.

God told Moses, "Stretch out your rod over the sea" (Exodus 14:16), and when he did, the water parted, and the people marched through to the other side. Then Moses stretched his rod out over the sea again; the waters closed and Pharaoh's army drowned. *Their obstacle became their means of deliverance.* The answer to their dilemma was in the dilemma itself. Your answer may lie in your dilemma, as well.

> Their obstacle became their means of deliverance.

For instance, when Jo Franz was told she had multiple sclerosis, she was devastated. She loved to sing and speak. But how could she continue her dream when she might eventually be confined to a wheelchair? What she didn't know then was that her disease would give her even more of a platform to speak of the power and strength of God in her weakness.

For Jim McClelland, following his Leader through his divorce gave him insight, credibility, and compassion, which he never would have had otherwise. These new gifts allow him to help people in his church even more. Now his life has been restored and given new joy, and he has found love in a new marriage. Life is good for him.

The children of Israel's answer was in the "impassable" river right in front of them. When they marched out onto dry land, Miriam picked up the tambourine and led them in song: "Sing to the LORD, for He has triumphed gloriously!" (Exodus 15:21 NIV).

If anyone knows about struggle, surely it would be Madame Guyon, who lived in France from 1648 to 1717. She was born into a religious and well-to-do home and was schooled in the convents. At age sixteen, she married an older man and during her twelve years of marriage, suffered terribly at the hands of her mother-in-law. Adding to her misery were the deaths of her half-sister, her mother, her son, and her daughter and father, who died within days of each other. During her marriage, she sought spiritual direction, and through her study came to believe she would be blessed despite suffering. She bore another son and daughter shortly before her husband's death, and became a widow at age twenty-eight.

In her continued study, she began to believe in salvation through grace, not works, and in the constant presence of God through prayer and inward stillness. She wrote about these ideas, which were considered heretical at the time by the church. The testimony of her brother, Father de La Motte, eventually sent her to prison in the Bastille for seven years,[3] a cruel betrayal. What could this woman know about your impossible situation? Consider her powerful words: "Courage, dear soul. You have come to the edge of the Red Sea, where soon you will see the enemy receive his reward. Follow on your present path. Remain immovable, like a rock. Do not find a pretext to stir from where you are. . . . The Lord will fight for you now. Many people break down at this place. They do not find the way out. They stop here and never advance. . . . That which is a rock of destruction to others is the port of safety to such a one."[4]

She was eventually released from prison and continued writing and her pursuit of spiritual direction. She would be amazed to know the scope of her influence throughout time and around the world. Fénelon (a spiritual director in King Louis the Fourteenth's court) became one of her disciples. Quakers have been influenced by her teachings on prayer. John Wesley, Charles Spurgeon, and Watchman Nee, among others, have all been influenced by the triumph of her life of persistent faith, no matter what the obstacle.

As you "follow on your present path"—one foot in front of the other—your faith, too, will be a light to others.

> *For this is . . . our God forever and ever;*
> *He will be our guide, even to death.*
> —PSALM 48:14

2. Feed Your Spiritual Self Daily

The children of Israel were used to being fed, and now there was no food for them in the wilderness. They complained to Moses, and God provided for them by sending bread from heaven called manna (it was like wafers of honey). Every morning (except the Sabbath), it fell from heaven. They were told to gather it daily—just enough for that day; except on the sixth day, they were to gather extra for the Sabbath. If they gathered more than they were directed, what was left over would rot.

"Give us this day our daily bread," Jesus taught us to pray. God promises to give us strength for the day, grace for the moment. We're not to anticipate sorrow or store up comfort for the future. Jesus said, "Sufficient for the day *is* its own trouble" (Matthew 6:34).

> We're not to anticipate sorrow or store up comfort for the future.

Our journey is a marathon, not a sprint.

Just as the Israelites needed daily manna, we need daily nourishment from God's Word. Reading the Bible is a discipline—just as physical exercise is a discipline—and it brings *life* to us.

Doug and Angela Tucker are pastors, and their whole life is

ministry. Surely that would make it easier for them to get into the Word regularly. Although their little guy, Samuel, was diagnosed as being terminal at birth, he is still living after ten years. Doug and Angela diligently care for him and faithfully tend to his daily needs, dealing with his occasional life-threatening health crises. But just because Doug and Angela are in spiritual leadership, that doesn't exempt them from discouragement and weariness of heart.

It has not been easy. Angela says it can be tempting to ignore the Word of God, stay home from church, and avoid relationships. She says, "I could just throw my hands in the air and say, 'I quit!' But God has been faithful to carry me as I pour my heart out to Him, drinking up His word and talking to Him as though He were sitting there with 'skin on.'"

> *Remember the word to Your servant*
> *upon which you have caused me to hope.*
> *This* is *my comfort in my affliction,*
> *for Your Word has given me life.*
> *Your Word* is *a lamp to my feet and a light to my path.*
> —PSALM 119:49, 50, 105

3. Look up to the Cross

As the children of Israel trudged through the wilderness, scripture says the "soul of the people became very discouraged on the way" (Numbers 21:4). They let loose a volley of complaints against Moses and God: "Why have you brought us up out of Egypt to die in the wilderness?" It didn't matter that they'd been miraculously provided with manna, with water from unlikely places, and with victory over their enemies—they still complained.

When they railed against the Lord, He sent deadly serpents that bit the people, and many of them died. The people quickly repented from speaking against the Lord (deadly biting serpents would certainly cure me of complaining!), and God told Moses to make a bronze serpent and put it on a pole. Anyone who looked up at the bronze serpent would live.

This is a strange and unusual story, but it tells a powerful truth. Jesus said, "As Moses lifted up the serpent in the wilderness, even so must the Son of Man be lifted up, that whoever believes in Him should not perish but have eternal life" (John 3:14, 15). Jesus became sin for us—and it is a watershed moment for each of us when we look on the cross, acknowledge our need of Him, and accept the redemption He offers. We look and live.

> It is a watershed moment for each of us when we look on the cross, acknowledge our need of Him, and accept the redemption He offers.

There's something deeply healing about the cross of Christ when you are suffering. He's experienced human suffering; he understands. He is touched by the feeling of our infirmities; He was wounded for our transgression, and by his stripes, we are healed (Isaiah 53:4–5). We actually enter into a special kind of fellowship with Christ when we suffer (Philippians 3:10). His example encourages us to go on: "Consider Him who endured such hostility, lest you become weary and discouraged in your souls" (Hebrews 12:3).

Suffering can be a stumbling block for many of us. We don't like it. And when we are confronted by the solution to our suffering—the cross—we turn away, not realizing that to look is to live. We do amazingly creative things to avoid pain.

Twelve days after Annabelle was born, her adoptive mom, Joan, came out with Annabelle for our first visit. While I was eager to see her, I was also dreading the visit. Amy was staying with us, healing from her C-section. I wondered, *Will seeing this precious baby tear the scab off the fresh wound? What will seeing her do to me? Can I take it?* That morning I had read in my devotional a passage from Isaiah 53. "We hid as it were our faces from Him." I knew there was an important truth in that passage.

The truth is I cannot "hide" from sorrow. Looking upon it is part of the healing, the redemption. If we turn away from it, it gives a foothold to shame. If we allow the truth of the cross to shine upon it, healing comes.

As it turned out, we had a precious visit, full of snuggles and sweet moments.

> *Let us fix our eyes on Jesus,*
> *the author and perfecter of our faith.*
> —HEBREWS 12:2 NIV

4. Set Your Heart on Pilgrimage

Setting your heart on pilgrimage is a different mind-set from setting your heart on a specific goal at a set point on the time line of life. The psalmist says it this way:

> Blessed *is* the man whose strength *is* in You,
> Whose heart is set on pilgrimage.
> *As they* pass through the Valley of Baca,
> They make it a spring; . . .
> They go from strength to strength (Psalm 84:5, 6)

Setting your heart on pilgrimage means keeping your heart set on moving forward. The path to recovery is a road, not a couch. Jesus said to the lame man, "Get up and walk."

> Setting your heart on pilgrimage means keeping your heart set on moving forward.

As the Israelites made their long pilgrimage through the wilderness, they had to get up and walk when God prompted them. They followed His lead and made the journey at His pace. They were guided by the cloud of Jehovah. Whenever the cloud lifted from above the Tabernacle tent, they knew it was time to set out on their journey. Whenever the cloud settled, the Israelites made camp.

Whether it was two days, a month, or a year that the cloud remained above the Tabernacle, the children of Israel would remain encamped and not journey; but when it was taken up, they would journey. At the command of the LORD they remained encamped, and at the command of the LORD they journeyed; they kept the charge of the LORD, at the command of the LORD by the hand of Moses (Numbers 9:22–23).

While God does not lead us directly—with a visible cloud that lifts and settles as He did the Israelites—He leads us nonetheless. Following His lead means staying the course, setting our hearts on completing the journey, and believing that He is a faithful and trustworthy guide.

Though the journey can be long, one of the great things about being a pilgrim on a pilgrimage is that you're not alone! Yes, God is with us on our pilgrimage, but there are other pilgrims on the path, too. Together, we keep going, no matter what, shoulder to shoulder.

Another pilgrimage blessing is that scattered along the way are oases with springs of living water. We may be passing through a valley of tears, but God will shower down sweet blessings as precious gifts. Our pilgrimage can seem never-ending, but the wilderness is a place we *pass through*. We don't have to make a home in the valley of tears. As we keep our hearts set on the pilgrimage, we keep moving *forward*.

One of the different things about a pilgrimage is that our journey can seem so ongoing and inconclusive. Yes, at times we do see answers to prayer; but oftentimes, the same person, the same situation rises back to the top of our prayer list. *Again.* It's hard to keep praying, keep looking for a breakthrough when it appears as if nothing is happening. We can be tempted to think, *Maybe things will never change. Maybe God isn't going to answer that prayer, so why keep on about it? What is the point?*

As with the Israelites' journey, we must remember that God's ways and timing are not our ways. Often the deep work He is doing is in *us*. Or perhaps the work He is doing is in our loved ones, and we must patiently stay the course. We do not know the whole picture yet.

As we continue on an often difficult journey, we must remember that *persistence pays*. If you look through Scripture, you will see that the people who came to Jesus were people like us. Here are some of their common threads:

- *Their needs were personal.* The people who came to Him often came on behalf of others. Some were mothers, fathers, or close friends. Some came to Him with their own needs. But whatever brought them, it was *personal*.

- *Jesus was their last hope.* In the story of the woman with the issue of blood, she'd spent all she had on physicians, but was no better. Jesus was her last hope (Mark 5:25–34). Then there was the father who had begged Jesus's disciples to help; but only Jesus could heal his epileptic son (Luke 9:37–42).

- *They were persistent in seeking answers from God.* Remember the parable of the persistent widow who had a legal problem (Luke 18:1–8)? Though the judge in the parable was slow to respond, she did not give up. Then there was the group of friends who cut a hole in a rooftop to lower their sick friend down in front of Jesus (Mark 2:1–12).

These desperate and persistent people had exhausted all of their other options and had no other place to go. They were stubborn in their faith, knowing that Jesus was their only answer, their only hope. They hung on to God with little or great faith, knowing He would provide, and their faith was rewarded. Their hearts were set on the pilgrimage.

As we look at the children of Israel as they made their way

from Egypt to Canaan, we see that not all their hearts were faithful. In fact, their complaints and rebellion were rampant. But they had good leaders whose hearts were in tune with God's, and with their help, the nation stayed its course. As we look to the hearts of Moses and Joshua, we find the strength to stay our own course as we walk through our wilderness and on to the promised peace.

> *In the wilderness you saw*
> *How the* LORD *your God carried you,*
> *As a man carries his son,*
> *in all the way you went until*
> *you came to this place.*
> —DEUTERONOMY 1:31

5. Keep Your Hope Alive

Joan Chittister, in her book *Scarred by Struggle*, poignantly describes the struggle of the broken, as we strive to keep hope alive: "It is not the struggle itself that lays us low. It is the day-in, day-out tenacious clinging to the amorphous anger, the depression, the unacceptability of it all that stands to defeat us in the end. When a loved one dies, we survive the death. The only question is whether or not we will survive dealing with the death. When the divorce we did not want comes anyway, we survive the separation. The question is whether or not we will survive the thought of having been left."[5]

Hope can defeat discouragement. Some of our situations are more impossible than others, but there is a powerful principle in being conscious of how we frame our circumstances: We can see with eyes of faith or with eyes of fear. We can see the possibility or the impossibility.

Even at the very start of their journey, the Israelites were blind to the possibilities and quickly lost heart. As they faced the Red

Sea, they were terrified: "And when Pharaoh drew near, the children of Israel lifted their eyes, and behold, the Egyptians marched after them. So they were afraid, and the children of Israel cried out to the LORD. Then they said to Moses, 'Because *there were* no graves in Egypt, have you taken us away to die in the wilderness?'" (Exodus 14:10–11)

Don't we sometimes do the same thing? At the first sign of defeat, we throw up our hands and think we are going to die!

It is a discipline to look for encouragement, to see the good in a dreary place. If no one else is encouraging you, take the initiative to encourage your own self. Jude writes, "But you, beloved, building yourselves up on your most holy faith . . . keep yourselves in the love of God" (Jude 1:20, 21).

The beautiful Three Sisters mountains that are near our home were named Faith, Hope, and Charity by the early settlers. "Hope" is the middle mountain, where there is a pass at the summit that can lead hikers *through*.

Hope can lead us through. When we place our hope in what can be, we choose to adopt the expectation that God will provide an answer even though we can't see it right away.

> When we place our hope in what can be, we choose to adopt the expectation that God will provide.

The psalmist asked himself, "Why are you cast down, O my soul? And why are you disquieted with me? Hope in God. . . . For I shall yet praise Him" (Psalm 43:5). *Hope reminds us of realities we can't yet see.* The reality is that because we are His, God is at work, no matter how it seems.

> *Therefore, my beloved brethren, be steadfast,*
> *immovable, always abounding in the work of the LORD*
> *knowing that your labor is not in vain.*
> —1 CORINTHIANS 15:58

6. Wait on God to Discern His Leading

There's an old song: "My Lord knows the way through the wilderness; all I have to do is follow." But how do we follow? We don't have a pillar of fire by night and a cloud by day, as the children of Israel did, nor do we have Moses up front, telling us where to go. We are left muddling through, trying to hear God's voice in often impossible situations.

Our family needed to hear God's will for Amy's precious baby. Plan A was out—Amy wasn't ready to be a mother. So what was plan B? We wanted to know. Countless nights I would awaken thinking, "What is your will, Father? Please, show us!"

Bill and I were distraught as we went through stacks of résumés of hopeful would-be parents with Amy and Jeff. So many families were aching for a child. We looked through beautiful scrapbooks of seemingly perfect families with glowing references. What about Fred and JoAnn? Or Sally and Brad? Or Justin and Brittany? *Pick us!*

There were times when we did, indeed, hear from God. But there were also times the silence was deafening, and our journey took us through many twists and turns. Looking back, the answer was right before our eyes, but as is often the case, sometimes God takes us to the brink. As we prayed, it seemed the Lord was saying, "Wait. I am at work. Be still."

Two months before Amy's due date, she and Jeff had finally chosen a family after many interviews and carefully checking references. We were impressed by how seriously they did their homework. They wanted a strong Christian family with a healthy marriage. It was a relief when they finally chose a couple, and the adoptive family came with us to the ultrasound. It was a girl *(I knew it!)*; and when I saw her image on the ultrasound, I exclaimed, "God has an incredible plan for this little one!" Maybe there was a plan, after all. We were all in tears as we saw the little image and heard her heart beating.

But only a few days later, the couple Amy and Jeff had chosen was told by their adoption agency that they were ineligible due to another recent adoption. We were all devastated. We thought we'd heard from God; but for whatever reason, the door was closed. Slammed shut. Now what? Were my husband and I supposed to keep the child? My heart said yes, my head said no.

> We thought we'd heard from God; but for whatever reason, the door was closed. Slammed shut. Now what?

Two days later, I slid into my Bible study a few minutes late. There was an empty seat next to Joan. I knew she and her husband had been trying to adopt and that a birth mother in another state had chosen them. "How's your adoption going?" I whispered.

She sighed and shook her head. "There were problems, so we withdrew. How's it going with Amy?"

"It just fell through." I sat back in my chair, wondering. *God? Is this You?*

Amy and Jeff had wanted to pursue Joan and Dirk from the very beginning, but we were concerned that an open adoption within the same church would be too close, so both families pursued other avenues. But now here we were, back to square one. We began to wonder if perhaps this was the path God wanted us to take. But how could we know? Amy suggested, "Maybe we can just sit down and talk with them."

At a dinner a few nights later, Amy and Jeff, Joan and Dirk, and Bill and I sat and talked openly about our dreams, desires, and concerns for this little one. Amy shared her heart for her baby, and we all wept. God was present. Here was our answer.

Even when we know in our hearts what God's will is, following it can sometimes be very scary. When the Israelites finally reached the borders of the land God had promised them, it was time to send in scouts to explore the land and see what was before them. However, the fear of the spies turned their hearts from following what they knew to be God's will. Their fear was contagious, and soon, all but a few faithful had set their minds in opposition to God's leading.

And there was a price to pay: "These men who have seen My glory and the signs which I did in Egypt and in the wilderness, and . . . have not heeded My voice, they certainly shall not see the land of which I swore to their fathers, nor shall any of those who rejected Me see it" (Numbers 14:22–23).

Trust and obedience to our heavenly Father means following through on what we discern His will to be. He is eager to show us the way and lead us to joy; ours is to follow.

> *But My servant Caleb, because he has a different spirit in him*
> *and has followed Me fully, I will bring into the land where he went,*
> *and his descendants shall inherit it.*
> —Numbers 14:24

7. Patiently Endure with Love

To endure means to remain firm under suffering or misfortune without yielding, to undergo a hardship without giving in.[6] Patient endurance is doing what love calls you to do. Paul wrote, "Love . . . always protects, always trusts, always hopes, always perseveres. Love never fails" (1 Corinthians 13:7, 8 NIV). Patient endurance is having the understanding that even though you may not be able to solve your delimma, you can do the right thing within the dilemma. Patient endurance is holding on to principles of love, respect, trust, and believing for the best, *no matter what.*

You can't go wrong with love. As we took steps to help our daughter relinquish her baby, we tried to keep these principles uppermost in our dealings.

> You can't go wrong with love.

During the relinquishment ceremony at the hospital, Amy placed her baby in the arms of Joan and Dirk. As she did that, they both wrapped their arms around Amy. Now as I look back, I see that they have indeed "wrapped" their arms around Amy and still give her respect and care.

At the relinquishment, we gave Joan and Dirk a Bible for Annabelle and one for their son, Wesley. I had their names imprinted on them, another step to say, "She is yours." It was painful to have the name ANNABELLE JOY ZELLER inscribed, but it was a necessary step, a moment of truth.

Now as over three years have passed, we are still focusing on the principles of love and respect, keeping them uppermost in our relationships. Initially, we had to focus on what would be best for Annabelle, even if that meant we would not see her. It could not be about us, not about our feelings, not about our "right" to be grandparents. It had to be all about Annabelle. That is the principle of love.

Has this always been easy for both families? No, at times it has been ragged, and we have often admitted that we're making it up as we go along. And yet, we are amazed at how beautifully God has worked in all of our lives. We never could have imagined we would have this little one so entrenched in our lives as well as in our hearts, along with her brother, Wesley, and the rest of the Zeller family. Loving Annabelle is a package deal. And it's a good one.

Annabelle and Wesley's adorable pictures smile at us from the refrigerator along with the rest of our seven adorable grandchildren. Looking back, we are grateful to see the hand of God. The original couple Amy and Jeff had chosen had to make a career move across the country, and we would have missed seeing her grow up.

After forty years of wandering, the Israelites finally got the reward of their endurance. As we've seen, their journey would have been shortened by nearly forty years had they trusted God from the beginning. However, not all "extended" wildernesses are our own doing. Sometimes, it just takes a long time to get through; other pilgrimages are much shorter. No matter the length of our journey, we will see the goodness of the Lord in the land of living (Psalm 27:13) if we patiently endure.

Do not throw away this confident trust in the LORD,
no matter what happens.
Remember the great reward it brings you!
Patient endurance is what you need now,
so you will continue to do God's will.
Then you will receive all that he has promised.
—HEBREWS 10:35, 36 NLT

8. Walk On!

Once the children of Israel got through the Red Sea, their journey was just beginning. For them to succeed, they needed to follow their leader, obey his direction, and keep their hopes set on getting to the Promised Land. Above all, their journey would take patient endurance and stubborn faith to believe that God would lead them.

Near our home is beautiful Canyon Creek Meadow, which lies near the summit of a rugged mountain. Several summers ago, Bill and I and some of our children decided to hike there, as we'd heard it was not to be missed—especially in late July. As we marched single file through a tunnel of trees, the path wound up and around for several miles through stands of tall trees. As we trudged upward, we were not always sure that we had stayed on the right course. The path itself was rocky and tedious.

When the kids grumbled about their aching legs or when one of us nearly twisted an ankle, I began to wonder if the effort was worth it. But then, just when I thought the trip had been a ridiculous waste of a summer Saturday, the fragrance of wildflowers filled the air. *How could this be?* I thought. *It's dark here. The sunlight is screened out by dense trees.* The floor of the forest was quiet and barren beneath the moss hanging from tall fir trees. But soon the path widened, and there it was: a beautiful, sun-drenched meadow fed by streams that cascaded from a glacier clinging to the side of the mountain.

The meadow was a mass of wildflowers of every variety, growing so thickly that the scene reminded me of an enormous English
garden. Enchanted, we took off our shoes and sat by the stream as
we ate our lunch, savoring our surroundings. All too soon it was
time to go back.

I have been back several times to this meadow, and each time I
am captivated by the beauty of Canyon Creek Meadow. It contin-
ues to remind me of the rewards of staying on the journey, of con-
tinuing the walk—one step at a time.

Certain times in my life are like the sun-drenched meadow;
beautiful moments, but rare! Many more times of my life are like
climbing up the mountain: exhausting, uncertain, painful, and tedious. Some days my writing and speaking seem as if they are going
nowhere. Marriage can be difficult. Parenting, while wonderful,
can mean worry and heartbreak. Business ventures can seem long
and complicated with little reward. Trying to be a real follower of
Jesus can feel obscure, as I ask, "Is my life really making a difference?"

> The longer I live, the more convinced I am that the struggle—the journey itself—is significant and necessary.

But the longer I live, the more convinced I
am that the struggle—the journey itself—is significant and necessary. For the "joy that was set
before Him," Jesus endured the cross (Hebrews
12:2). Endurance is a difficult path, and often it's
lonely. And yet struggle is honest and very, very
human.

Joan Chittister writes, "Endurance is . . .
commitment to whatever makes life worthwhile.
It is the willingness to keep on doing what must be done because
doing it is meaningful, is worthy of us, and more than equals the
struggle it takes to do it. . . . We can endure anything for the sake
of the things we love. We can endure years at a bedside, years of
study, a lifetime of practice, a career of service, the denial of good
things we consider less worthy than the things we really care about.
Endurance is the sacrament of commitment. . . . We are given the
gift of endurance for the sake of the great things of life."[7]

Perhaps there is something in your life now that is a struggle for you—even though you know you are where you should be—and you are tempted to give up. The biggest battle we must win is with our own selves. Many voices today would tell you that nobody should have to work this hard, that nothing is worth this kind of pain. But the battle is won not so much in blinding moments of truth as in hanging in there when the going is tough. *Don't give up!* If you are following the Lord, your path will ultimately lead you to a beautiful place. Meanwhile, keep going.

> If you are following the Lord, your path will ultimately lead you to a beautiful place.

Open your eyes to His presence in the midst of your struggle and stay the course.

Since we are surrounded by such a great cloud of witnesses,
let us throw off everything that hinders
and the sin that so easily entangles,
and let us run with perseverance the race marked out for us.
Let us fix our eyes on Jesus, the author and perfecter of our faith,
who for the joy set before him endured the cross, scorning its shame,
and sat down at the
right hand of the throne of God.
Consider him who endured such opposition from sinful men,
so that you will not grow weary and lose heart.
—HEBREWS 12:1–3 NIV

PERSONAL REFLECTION

Read the story of Moses and the exodus from Egypt (see Exodus, chapters 13–19). What do you think kept Moses motivated to keep going?

1. Ask yourself, "What is the hardest thing right now about my journey? What steps must I take to persevere?"
2. What is my obstacle?
3. Using the metaphor of the Red Sea, how can my obstacle become my means of deliverance?
4. How can I rethink my "obstacle," see it in a new light?
5. If I am facing a dilemma (no easy answers), what is the right thing I can do right now within my dilemma?

To inspire yourself, list some positive, hope-affirming goals to keep you going in the right direction.

NEW BEGINNINGS RESOURCE

Steps to Get You Started

- List positive, hope-affirming goals to keep you going in the right direction.
- Read chapters 20 through 33 of Jeremiah.
- In your prayer journal, write ways to encourage your own self (Jude 20).
- Think of ways to "feed" your hopes and new dreams.

Recommended Reading

Holding on to Hope by Nancy Guthrie (study of book of Job)
Scarred by Struggle, Transformed by Hope by Joan D. Chittister
*Praying for Your Prodigal Daughter: Hope, Help & Encourage-
     ment for Hurting Parents* by Janet Thompson
The Best Life Ain't Easy by Virelle Kidder

I heard two meadow larks again this spring,
calling and responding
to each other on a cold and windy day.
God began to speak to me through them.
I heard them urging me to keep my own summer song,
even though life's winter tries to throw
into my spring cold wind and snow.
Do not throw away your confidence, he said.
Do not budge from your perch, but sing your song,
summer confident,
sure of my great goodness for you.
You did not bring this spring, dear child,
you do not have to arrange for the summer to follow.
They come from the Father's will and they will come.

—John Eldredge, *Journey of Desire*[1]

CHAPTER EIGHT

Spiritual Strategy #5: Sing a New Song

Yᴏᴜ ᴡᴏᴜʟᴅ ᴛʜɪɴᴋ that while you're going through hard times, you should be exempt from the little, niggling things. But that's usually not how life works. The dryer breaks. The pipes freeze, and the electricity goes off. The dog gets into the garbage and then gets sick from eating it. The pressure of meeting budgets, deadlines, and family expectations is constantly with us. As I write, it is Christmas, and I am facing a writing deadline.

Christmas is coming whether I'm ready for it or not (that means nineteen of us for several days). There's a story in the Bible (2 Chronicles 20) about a time when the Israelites discovered that enormous armies were coming to wipe them out. They were completely outnumbered, and their leader, Jehosaphat, didn't know what to do: "We have no power against this great multitude that is coming against us; nor do we know what to do, but our eyes are upon You" (2 Chronicles 20:12).

As I read how Jehosaphat and his people felt overwhelmed at the thought of a formidable enemy, I thought, *That's kind of how I feel: Christmas is marching toward me, and there's no way I can buy the perfect gift for everyone, fix that not-to-be-missed dish, write the cards, get to all the Christmas programs. And stay in budget! Not to mention meet my writing deadline.*

Okay, so it's pretty weak to compare my Christmas anxieties to what Jehosphat was experiencing. But being overwhelmed by life's challenges, big or small, can be enough to make any of us lose our song.

> Being overwhelmed by life's challenges, big or small, can be enough to make any of us lose our song.

As Jehosaphat faced his very formidable enemy, the only weapon he put in his army's possession was *praise*. Before they trooped into battle, Jehosaphat commissioned men to sing praises to God as they marched. No weapons—only praise and singing. And in the confusion, their enemies fought each other and all were destroyed. It was an amazing victory. From this battle—and from this victory—we learn seven powerful spiritual strategies to guide us through our own crises. And every one of them is centered in the concept of *singing a song of praise and gratitude.*

1. Get a Word from God

Things looked bad for Jehosaphat and his country. Fatal, in fact. His first response was to gather everyone together for a time of fasting and prayer. Jehosaphat said, "We must hear from God." In his public prayer, he stated honestly that he did not know what to do and declared his utter dependence upon God. Then he waited for a word from God.

While some crises leave us with only one choice—survival—others present us with multiple choices, and we don't know which one is the best.

Karen and her husband faced a dilemma when their newly married daughter had a mental break and was diagnosed with schizoaffective disorder. How should they support their new son-in-law? What should their parenting role be now?

How do you get a word from God? You read the Bible. And you pray—gut-level, honest, throw-yourself-on-his-mercy prayers. Fasting prayers. During our family's dilemma, we knew we had to get a word from God as to how to proceed. And it seemed the answer we got from God was, "*Wait*." Something I find extremely difficult.

The children of Israel and Jehosaphat got their word from God through Jahaziel, one of the sons of the Levites, a worship leader. They were given an unusual strategy: take your position, stand firm, and see God's deliverance.

How do you know when to struggle, to try to solve something, to fix it—and when to back off and let the Lord fight your battle? Here's a word from God: "After you have done everything . . . stand" (Ephesians 6:10–13). There are times to stand on what you know and worship God right then and there. Many years ago, the old Scottish preacher G. Campbell Morgan wrote, "When the work presses, and the battle thickens, and the day seems long in coming, it is good for the heart to remember that the present conflict is with defeated foes.[2]

> Being objective in how we see the facts is important, but how we frame them is even more important.

> *This is what the LORD says to you:*
> *"Do not be afraid or discouraged because of this vast army.*
> *For the battle is not yours, but God's. . . .*
> *You will not have to fight this battle.*
> *Take up your positions; stand firm and see the deliverance*
> *the LORD will give you, O Judah and Jerusalem.*
> *Do not be afraid; do not be discouraged.*
> *Go out to face them tomorrow, and the LORD will be with you.*
> —2 CHRONICLES 20:15, 17 NIV

2. Check Your Attitude

Certainly facts are important—the hard, cold facts. Jehosaphat didn't minimize the crisis they were in. He took their situation seriously enough that he called his people together and led them in fasting and prayer. Being objective in how we see the facts is important, but how we frame them is even more important.

I tend to see my cup as half-empty rather than half-full. I was in despair over my daughter and the tiny baby developing in her womb, and I did a lot of hand-wringing. *This was the only flesh and blood she knew in the world. Whatever were we going to do?* Amy wasn't ready to be a mother, and we knew we had to help her with her hard choice. I was consumed with concern.

One day Bill grew exasperated with my anguish, and he said, "Nancie, you can make this event a blessing, a joy, and see God's hand in it; or you can continue to see the worst." I knew I had a choice, but his words made me angry. I retorted, "Well, I'm not used to giving up my grandbabies!"

But I knew he was right. He was grieving, too, while trying to support Amy and Jeff, who were doing the hardest thing they'd ever done. It was hard for our whole family.

How can you be joyful in impossible circumstances? The truth is, attitude makes all the difference, and we can adjust our attitude to fit the facts.

Minister and psychologist Ann Kaiser Stearns has interviewed and studied survivors from all sorts of tragedies. She lists the following as attitudes crucial for overcoming adversity:

- I will not be defeated.
- I will vividly examine the future.
- I will take advantage of available opportunities.
- I will accept life's challenges.
- I have to be willing to expand.
- I am consciously deciding to be in the company of good people.[3]

When Paul the Apostle said, "I can do all things through Christ who strengthens me" (Philippians 4:13), this was not a glib, grandiose statement. As I read the full context, it seems to me that his faith statement was not based on a belief that "I can accomplish anything I decide to put my mind to." No, it was a humble, graceful acceptance of where he was. He said, "I can abase and abound." In other words, I can gracefully be in need and receive help from other people. And I can gracefully succeed and give to others. I know how to suffer. I know how to have joy. I can lose, because ultimately, "I know whom I have believed and am persuaded that He is able to keep what I have committed to Him until that Day (2 Timothy 1:12).

This is the same Paul who, after preaching with Silas, was beaten and put in stocks and thrown into a dungeon for preaching the gospel. And what was Paul and Silas' response to their mistreatment? At midnight, they began singing and praising God. An earthquake shook the building, released their chains, and they were set free. Then they were able to lead the jailer and his family to faith in Christ (Acts 16:16–34).

Praise has the power to free us—not from the circumstances we find ourselves in, but from being consumed by our sadness and loss.

> *My brethren, count it all joy when you fall into various trials,*
> *knowing that the testing of your faith produces patience.*
> *But let patience have its perfect work,*
> *that you may be perfect and complete, lacking nothing.*
> *If any of you lacks wisdom, let him ask of God,*
> *who gives to all liberally and without reproach,*
> *and it will be given to him.*
> —JAMES 1:2–5

3. Associate with Praising, Positive People

Jehosaphat's people walked out shoulder to shoulder, to meet their enemy, singing. They carried no weapons. They simply praised. There is power in praise; Scripture even says that God inhabits the praises of his people. When we choose to praise, we choose to enter his presence. Praise helps us transcend our circumstances.

Praise is also contagious. Think of someone you know, whom everybody loves to be around. Why? Usually it's because he or she makes you smile. They're fun. They're optimistic and anything is possible. They're usually up for an adventure and tend to see the positive, not the negative. The world is starving for people like this, and there are just not enough of them to go around. If you don't naturally have this quality, try to cultivate it. My three sisters, Janie, Judy, and Kitty, are positive people with great senses of humor, and just being with them for an hour or two somehow helps to put my world back together because we laugh so much. Our problems and challenges always seem more manageable when we're able to laugh with each other. There is great strength in joy. Corrie ten Boom said, "Worry does not empty tomorrow of its sorrow; it empties today of its strength."[4]

Surround yourself with people of faith and ask for their prayers. This is no time for pride. Jehosphat knew he couldn't confront the challenge he was facing alone, and he gathered his people together to pray.

When you're going through a trial, gather your prayer troops. Our family was shameless about asking for prayer from our friends and family. How do people survive unbearable circumstances? For us, I can tell you that God's arms were around us through the prayers of our children and other people of faith. That can be true for you, too.

4. Choose to Walk in Praise and Joy

What makes one story a triumph and another a tragedy?

Sarah and Christine both had difficult childhoods. Sarah continued to have a difficult life; she divorced twice and never could seem to find happiness. She is often critical, and people tend to avoid her.

Christine, on the other hand, has worked hard to make a good life. She married and raised a family and became an artist. She has had her share of disappointments, but she always sees the best, and people love to be around her. What is the difference? It's called "point of view." It's the lens through which we choose to see life: we can view life as a raw deal, or we choose to see the good things and be grateful. We can see the possibilities or see the impossibilities. We choose what we see, what we focus on.

As Eugene Peterson tells us, "We cannot make ourselves joyful. Joy cannot be commanded, purchased, or arranged. But there is something we can do. We can decide to live in response to the abundance of God, and not under the dictatorship of our own poor needs. We can decide to live in the environment of a living God and not our own dying selves."[5]

We are often emotion-driven and tend to think we are what we feel. But that is not true. We can decide to let God's peace be in charge: "Let the peace of God rule in your hearts . . . and be thankful" (Colossians 3:15). What we see right now is not the end of the story. There is joy ahead. Living with joy is a decision we make.

My friend Caro, who went through breast cancer and complications from treatments for several years, declares, "Suffering is inevitable; misery is optional!"

Praise brings a fresh perspective. One late afternoon I'd been working long and hard at my computer and I needed to get out of the house, but the weather was dreary and uninviting. Although we live near the mountains, we cannot see them from our house, as we're surrounded by trees. To see the mountains, I must walk to the meadow. I was not only tired of the weather, I was tired of my life.

I put on my jacket and gloves and tromped through the trees, hurrying before it got dark. The air held just the hint of a thaw, and I heard the sound of an early red-winged blackbird. Before long, I reached the meadow, and sure enough, there were the mountains. I stopped and caught my breath. The breathtakingly blue sky was spectacular with the sun setting on the great billowing clouds and the mountains. The brilliant colors of purple and silver and white were like an artist's exotic palette.

I stopped and simply took in the view. *Thank you,* I breathed. I thought of the psalmist's description: "Clouds and darkness surround Him; righteousness and justice *are* the foundation of His throne. The heavens declare His righteousness, And all the peoples see His glory" (Psalms 97:2, 6). As I walked, I began to pray again for a need that had been bothering me for some time, and then I stopped. This time, instead of pleading and petitioning God as I usually did, I began to praise him. And as I did, my discontent and concerns seemed to fade in the light of his magnificent creation. Suddenly the birds that seemed incidental before my walk were now the focus, and I was amazed to see tiny buds on a willow tree. I was reminded of Jesus' words, "Look at the birds of the air . . . your heavenly Father feeds them. Are you not of more value than they?" (Matthew 6:26).

> This time, instead of pleading and petitioning God as I usually did, I began to praise him.

As I slowly walked through the meadow, I was aware that my depression had lifted. What had changed? Nothing—yet everything. My life was the same with the same needs, but as I walked in praise, I was in a new place. My point of view had changed.

Jehosaphat had the wisdom to know that as his people marched toward their enemy, the choice to offer praise as they journeyed would strengthen their hearts.

It is one thing to come to church and sing the praise songs, but it is another to *live* with an attitude of praise and worship. It's simple and yet profound. Deuteronomy 30:14 says, "But the word *is* very near you, in your mouth and in your heart." Praise comes from an honest heart of obedience, a recognition of God's powerful presence, and a faith that He's in control. Not that everything is wonderful. It is, after all, a *sacrifice* of praise that we bring (Hebrews 13:15). But He is worthy of our praise because He is the Redeemer. He redeems all things. And He is faithful. How can we *not* praise Him? "I will bless the Lord at all times,"

David sang, "His praise shall continually be in my mouth" (Psalms 34:1).

There is a captivating story in Matthew 15 that tells of a Canaanite woman who had a demon-possessed daughter. Jesus had his hands full with the people he was already trying to reach, but she wouldn't let him alone until he healed her daughter. She was an annoyance to the disciples who just wanted to get rid of her. The account says that Jesus did not answer a word to the woman, in spite of her pleading. And yet *even in Jesus' silence*, she worshiped Him. Her faith was irresistible to Jesus, and He exclaimed, "O woman, great *is* your faith! Let it be to you as you desire" (Matthew 15:28).

> We tend to think about what we *should* have, rather than what we *do* have.

Do we worship God, even in His silence? Like this persistent woman, we can persistently believe that He is our only hope and worship Him, even when we don't hear His song in return. Faith says, "Hold on. Believe what seems impossible. He is able. He is faithful. He cannot deny Himself."

> *Rejoice always, pray without ceasing.*
> *In everything give thanks,*
> *for this is the will of God in Christ Jesus concerning you.*
> *Make your requests known unto*
> *God with thanksgiving,*
> *and the peace of God which passes understanding*
> *shall keep your hearts and minds through Christ Jesus.*
> —I THESSALONIANS 5:16–18

5. Cultivate Gratitude

Fallen creatures that we are, we tend to think about what we *should* have, rather than what we *do* have, what could go *wrong* instead of what could go *right*. And sometimes we even pray that way—with worry instead of with faith. When we're problem oriented in our thinking, it increases our worry. For some of us more than others, it takes a conscious choice to be grateful. After all, one of the first things we teach our children to say is "thank you." Gratitude usually doesn't come naturally.

My mother was a charming person, and I think the fact that she was filled with gratitude made her that way. She had a brilliant, quick mind, but we lost her to Alzheimer's disease—that long, slow good-bye. One weekend when the disease was taking its toll on her, we kept her at our house. I was amazed to see that of all the times in her life when she could have been bitter or angry, Mother was instead overwhelmingly grateful. Grateful for her family. Grateful for God's beautiful world. Grateful for the canned soup I heated her for lunch. ("Oh, this is wonderful, Nancie!") I felt guilty; it seemed such a small thing.

I gulped down my soup and rushed on to my "to do" list, impatiently curtailing my activities and responsibilities to fit Mother's slower pace as she focused on a flower, the sunshine, my daughter's face cupped in her hands. My mother taught me many things; and now, in what had to be one of the most difficult phases of her life, she showed me that it's possible to have a heart of gratitude toward God in all circumstances.

When God gave Jehosaphat and the Israelites a great victory, they assembled together and praised God in gratitude.

> Maybe we don't really see what we have until we see what we have lost.

Gratitude gets lost when we don't see the beauty and goodness in everyday life, even in the difficult times. Sometimes it takes a conscious effort to be grateful. And maybe we don't really see what we have until we see what we have lost.

Having a heart of praise automatically increases our thankfulness. Henri Nouwen said this:

To be grateful for the good things that happen in our lives is easy, but to be grateful for all of our lives—the good as well as the bad, the moments of joy as well as the moments of sorrow, the successes as well as the failures, the rewards as well as the rejections—that requires hard, spiritual work. Still, we are only grateful people when we can say thank you to all that has brought us to the present moment. . . . Let's not be afraid to look at everything that has brought us to where we are now and trust that we will soon see in it the guiding hand of a loving God.[6]

Once we open our hearts to see the blessings God gives, we will be amazed and charmed by how rich and full life is. As we see that God is, indeed, good, we will be filled with gratitude.

> *Oh that men would give thanks to the* LORD *for His goodness,*
> *and for His wonderful works to the children of men!*
> *For He satisfies the longing soul,*
> *and fills the hungry soul with goodness.*
> —PSALM 107:8, 9

6. Tap into the Healing Power of Laughter

In Norman Cousins' book *Anatomy of an Illness*, he tells how he made a remarkable recovery from a potentially fatal illness. With his doctor's cooperation, he began doing research to develop a plan for his recovery. He learned that positive emotions have positive effects on the body, so he began to fight the pain with laughter. He rented funny movies and discovered that one ten-minute interlude of laughter produced two hours of painless sleep. It also reduced inflammation. He continued to improve, and more than a decade later, he was completely restored.[7]

> He learned that positive emotions have positive effects on the body.

Here are some verses that tell us what God says about the importance of laughter:

- A merry heart does good, *like* medicine (Proverbs 17:22).
- A joyful heart makes a cheerful face (Proverbs 15:13).

- A cheerful heart has a continual feast (Proverbs 15:15).
- For I will turn their mourning into joy, and will comfort them, and give them joy for their sorrow (Jeremiah 31:13).

Again, we turn to Henri Nouwen for some incredible insight. "I will thank [God] for the pleasures given me through my senses, for the glory of the thunder, for the mystery of music, the singing of the birds and the laughter of children. Truly, O Lord, the earth is full of thy riches!"[8]

Sometimes you just have to laugh at yourself. Last Sunday it was Bill's and my turn to pick up his parents for church (Dad is ninety-seven; Mom is eighty-seven). It was a special Christmas service, and we were looking forward to being there with the family. We also had our son Eric, his wife Carly, and their two sons, ages two and four, with us. In an effort to be festive, I grabbed my black velvet scarf out of my drawer and threw it over my red sweater. We straggled into church—walkers, kids, and all. I finally sat down to savor the service. Something kept tickling my neck, and I reached up to discover a black pair of pantyhose, dangling down the front of my sweater. They had been stuck to my scarf. Horrified, I stuffed them into my purse, but not before an usher, a good friend of ours, noticed. *Laughter is good!*

George MacDonald reminds us, "It is the heart that is not yet sure of its God that is afraid to laugh in his presence."[9]

> *[He gives us] beauty for ashes, the oil of joy for mourning,*
> *The garment of praise for the spirit of heaviness.*
> —ISAIAH 61:3

7. Count Your Blessings

Count your blessings. You'll find that there are many when you start making a list! There's an old song that says, "Count your blessings, name them one by one. And it will surprise you what the Lord has done."

It is a refreshing exercise to literally sit down with a notebook and begin to list your blessings. One day when I was feeling down, I wrote Philippians 4:8 at the top of a page: "Whatever things are true, noble, just, pure, lovely, good report." Under each category, I began to list the true things, the noble things, the just things, and so on. Before long, I filled several pages. And the old song was right, it did surprise me how many blessings I had.

When we count our blessings, it helps us let go of the worries and negatives in our lives. It also keeps us from being consumed by the problem or the problem-person. It shifts our focus and brings color and joy to our lives.

The Israelites' enemies were defeated as they turned on themselves and destroyed each other as the Israelites simply stood . . . and walked . . . and sang . . . and praised. The name of the valley where the enemy was defeated is Berachah, which in Hebrew means "praise," or "blessing." So instead of being a place of defeat, the valley became a place of blessing.

Amy got married in the summer of 2006, and she was such a beautiful bride. *Blessings!* I sat in the front row and counted my blessings: dear extended family and friends, my four wonderful, supportive sons: Jon, Eric, Chris, and Andy, so handsome; my daughters-in-law: Brittni, Carly, Jami, and Michelle, all four of them Amy's bridesmaids, beautiful inside and out; our adorable grandchildren, the light of our lives. I saw Bill, my faithful, committed husband of forty years, give away our daughter to our new son-in-law, Jeff, who truly loves Amy, and then I watched Bill perform the ceremony. I saw Amy's gorgeous baby, Annabelle, who was the honorary flower girl, there in the front row with her adoptive family, Joan and Dirk, who love her so, and who are committed to succeeding as parents. We are so blessed to have Annabelle in our lives—as well as her family. So many, many, blessings! It is amazing how love grows. It is amazing how God makes a way when there seems to be no way. I have so many blessings, it makes me want to *sing*!

Whatever things are true, whatever things are noble,
whatever things are just, whatever things are pure,
whatever things are lovely, whatever things are of good report,
if there is any virtue and if there is anything praise-worthy
—meditate on these things.
—PHILIPPIANS 4:8

PERSONAL REFLECTION

Read the story of Jehosaphat in 2 Chronicles 20.

1. Go back and read his prayer in verses 5 through 12.

2. When have you most felt overwhelmed by life? What factors made it seem so overwhelming?

3. See 2 Chronicles 20:15–17. In your own words, what was the "word of God" to the people? How does that inspire your own faith?

Read Psalms 103 and 104 and from those psalms, list things for which you can thank the Lord.

1. Get a small notebook (call it your "gratitude" or "blessing" journal), and once a week, record five things for which you are grateful.

2. Be intentional about expressing appreciation for someone or something every day.

3. Think of someone who has inspired you, and make a point of writing a note to that person.

<u>Choose Happiness</u>

Recent studies in Britain as well as in America conclude that happiness is contagious. Happiness also has a protective effect on your immune system so that you produce fewer stress hormones.[10]

Make conscious choices to spend time with happy people. Cultivate a sense of humor. Find books and movies that make you laugh. Rent the movie *Babette's Feast* and enjoy the life-affirming message it brings. If you don't have one, "borrow" a four-year-old for the day, and you will get a whole fresh perspective on life!

Recommended Reading:

This Is Your Brain on Joy—A Revolutionary Program for Balancing Mood, Restoring Brain Health, and Nurturing Spiritual Growth by Earl Henslin and Daniel Amen

You Gotta Keep Dancin'—In the Midst of Life's Hurts, You Can Choose Joy by Tim Hansel

But Joy Comes in the Morning—Studies on Peace by Max Lucado

Soar Unafraid by Jo Franz

Life and faith always insist on moving forward—
and I cannot move forward
without leaving something behind . . .
and possibly the most difficult to let go are
treasuries of painful experiences.

—Paul Tournier, *A Place for You*[1]

CHAPTER NINE

Spiritual Strategy #6: *Let Go, so God Can Hold You Close*

SOMETIMES YOU LET go, and sometimes things are ripped from you: the marriage you did not want to end; a job that was more than a job to you; your health that fails no matter what you do; a loved one, gone through death or separation. These new realities are hard to accept. But after the grieving, if we are to experience healing, we must let go. Life is about moving forward, and somehow we must let go of the past.

Sometimes we have to let go of good things as well as bad. It's possible to get stuck on past successes or the good old days. I sometimes long for the time when all my children were home or for the adrenaline days of when my husband and I were publishing magazines. They were great years, though filled with stress and challenges. But the challenge is: how do we live today?

Frederick Buechner knew the importance of looking forward: "What quickens my pulse now is the stretch ahead rather than the one behind, and it is mainly for some clue as to where I am going that I search through where I have been, for some hint as to who I am becoming or failing to become that I delve into what used to be."[2]

In a poem about his maturing son, C. Day Lewis wrote,

I have had worse partings, but none that so
Gnaws at my mind still. Perhaps it is roughly
Saying what God alone could perfectly show—
How selfhood begins with a walking away,
And love is proved in the letting go.[3]

Sometimes we pretend that our people—our spouses, our children, our family and friends—are ours. They are not. They are God's. They are in our custody to love, to pray for, to cherish. They are a temporary trust, which we hold loosely. And so, there are times when we have to let go of the people we love.

Let Go of People

Some years ago, my firstborn son, Jon—who was eighteen at the time—came into my office, excited to tell me about something that had happened at his summer job as a lifeguard. But that's Jon—always excited about something. He would be leaving for college in just a few weeks. I remember thinking how handsome and healthy he looked, and my mind flashed back to his first day of school. He was infinitely precious—with his white-blond hair, his new navy-blue jacket and jeans, and holding his new pencil box with new crayons and pencils inside.

And now he was leaving home. He was so eager to go to college. How could I not be glad for him? But how could I let him go? There are no lessons on how to do that.

There were to be several other "letting go" moments as a mom, and they are each still vividly etched in my mind: driving Eric to California to start school; helping Chris pack for his freshman year of college; Andy backing out of the driveway, his little car jammed full of clothes and dorm furnishings; waving out our car window as we left Amy at the doorway of a tiny apartment where she was trying her wings.

Fast-forward to a June Tuesday. I was in Target, buying gifts for the family who was adopting my daughter's baby. They were taking Annabelle home from the hospital that very day. My granddaughter. I bought Wesley, their four-year-old son, a Spider-Man truck. As I paid, the clerk said, "Have a great day!"

I went next door into Macy's and got lotion and a small gift for Amy. As the clerk puts the items in a bag, she said, "Now, you have a wonderful day." *Okay, lady, I'll try.* Then I went into the baby section to pick out a little outfit for Annabelle—a blanket, a picture for her wall. The clerk commented with a smile, "Someone has a new baby girl . . ."

"Yes," I answered.

As I left, she said, "Have a good day!" I wanted to scream, *I am NOT having a good day!* A sense of being utterly alone hit me. It was a day of letting go.

> I wanted to scream, I am NOT having a good day!

Each child fills a place that is irreplaceable. And yes, they do come back, but in a different way.

As I write, I am acutely aware that some of you reading this have lost a child whom you will never see graduate from college, or get married, or have children of their own. That is a loss I can barely comprehend.

The Old Testament character Jacob knew that loss. His son Joseph—who reminded him so of his wife, Rachel—turned up missing one day. The older brothers came home with Joseph's coat of many colors, covered in animal blood. Joseph was gone. Surely he'd been torn to pieces. Jacob had no way of knowing what had really happened to Joseph—that his older brothers had sold him into slavery. He didn't know Joseph's fate until years later. Meanwhile, he was left with his grief and empty questions: "What happened? Where is Joseph?"

It seemed that everything Jacob held dear had been taken from him: His beautiful Rachel had died giving birth to Joseph's baby brother as they had journeyed to their new home. Jacob had no choice but to bury her along the way and keep going (Genesis 35). And now Joseph was missing, not even a body to bury.

Whom have I in heaven but You? And there is none upon earth
that I desire besides You. My flesh and my heart fail;
But God is the strength of my heart and my portion forever.
—PSALM 73:25, 26

Let Go of Unforgiveness

Forgiving Others

While Jacob was grieving the loss of his son, Joseph was also suffering great loss. When his older brothers sold him into slavery at the tender age of seventeen, he lost everything—his home, his father, and his little brother, Benjamin. He lost his freedom and the potential of his future. In Egypt, however, Joseph managed to land on his feet and ended up in leadership in Potiphar's house. But things turned sour for Joseph when Potiphar's wife went after him and Joseph rebuffed her advances. Furious, she lied that Joseph had pursued her, and Joseph was thrown in prison. Another betrayal.

While in prison, Joseph used his spiritual gift to interpret dreams, which resulted in one of his fellow prisoners—a butler—being set free. Though the butler had promised to remember him to Pharaoh, he forgot Joseph, and Joseph stayed in prison two more years. More betrayal.

But when Pharaoh had a troubling dream that none of his seers could interpret, the butler suddenly remembered Joseph, who was still in prison for something he did not do. When Joseph correctly interpreted Pharaoh's dream, Pharaoh quickly recognized Joseph's value and put him in a position to help Egypt survive the coming famine. Not long after, Joseph's brothers showed up in Egypt, begging for food. They did not recognize Joseph, but Joseph recognized them.

Joseph had a choice to make. He had multiple reasons to be angry and resentful, but he chose instead to *forgive*. Through every step of his difficult journey, Joseph maintained his faith in God and used the gifts God had given him.

It was his willingness to forgive others that allowed Joseph to move on. It was his commitment to never stop loving, no matter what. It was his unwavering grasp of the truth that God had a bigger purpose that could even embrace his brothers' betrayal (Genesis 40–45).

Forgiving others frees you from the bondage of the past. Though you may not forget, you can let go and forgive. Yes, it's true that your past is powerful and life-shaping. But like Joseph, you need not let it defeat you or define you.

> Forgiving others frees you from the bondage of the past.

God's ways are not our ways. His larger purposes can transcend life. Joseph said later to his brothers, "Do not be afraid . . . as for you, you meant evil against me; but God meant it for good, in order to bring it about as it is this day, to save many people alive . . . ' And he comforted them and spoke kindly to them" (Genesis 19–21).

Forgiving Ourselves

As important as it is to forgive others, we must forgive ourselves, too. I've lain awake too many nights thinking, *Why didn't we get help earlier?* Or, *If only we'd intervened, we may not be in this place.* It's called "beating yourself up"—a fruitless exercise. Stop! Easier said than done, I know. But it is possible to let go as we keep revisiting forgiveness.

One morning as I dressed, I noticed a little silver chain necklace on my dresser where it had lain for several weeks. On the chain are two tiny silver drops on which these two words are engraved: *best grandma*. It's one of my favorite necklaces, given to me by my son and daughter-in-law, but I realized I had not been wearing it lately. It suddenly occurred to me why: it was because I felt I didn't deserve the label. I put it on anyway, and a voice hit me out of nowhere, *How could you?* My own voice, a voice of accusation: *A good grandmother would never give up her grandchild!*

I was stunned to recognize this attitude in myself. I thought I was past it. We'd done the best we could, and were trying to go on. But on this day, I knew I needed to revisit forgiveness. *Again*. I needed to let it go.

Guilt, anger, and shame can be so deeply ingrained in our hearts that they color everything in our lives, and we're not even aware they are there. But they weigh us down and keep us from joyfully running the race God has set before us.

When we are confronted by the ugly presence of these emotions, we must realize that the harsh voice of bitterness and condemnation is not God's voice—it is the voice of the enemy of our soul, the accuser of God's children. And we must not agree with him. Even when we've made mistakes, if we have asked forgiveness from God and others for real or perceived failings, then we must let it go. Leave it. But often the last person we let off the hook is our own selves. That's what I had to do—I needed to forgive myself.

> Often the last person we let off the hook is our own selves.

We can spend a lot of time trying to fix what went wrong. But we cannot heal the deepest hurts. Only God can. And only we can allow Him to do it. Forgiveness is the only answer when we have no other answer.

My friend Nancy Tushabe helps her husband run orphanages in Uganda and knows a lot about families and loving and loss. When I told her how we helped our daughter place her child for adoption, she said to me, "Oh my, there's got to be a lot of forgiveness."

At the time, I did not know how much. Now, as I fastened the necklace around my neck, I said silently, *Nancy, you are right. There has had to be a lot of forgiveness. And the person I most need to forgive is myself.*

Perhaps it's difficult to let go of our painful experience because of the people it represents. We don't want to let go of our loved one. In a way, letting go can seem like losing him or her again.

But letting go is an important step to wholeness and healing. It's been said that "forgiveness . . . is a willingness to get over what you think should have happened and an acceptance of the reality of what actually happened."[4]

While on our visit to Amy's birth country, Amy and I stood in front of a traditional Korean house in a coastal city in South Korea. Our guide said, "I think this is the place." The place where Amy—Yung Ja—had been left as a three-month-old baby. Amy and I stood together in silent awe. This was where my daughter had begun the adventure that led her to us.

I wondered who brought Amy here. Was it her mother, Soon Ja? Was it her grandmother? Or her grandfather? Did they know the people who lived here? No one seemed to know anything. I reasoned that it might have been Amy's grandmother—Soon Ja's mother—who brought Amy to this door, leaving her with orders to take her to the orphanage. And if so, I wanted to ask her, *What were you thinking? Children shouldn't be left. Mothers and grandmothers aren't supposed to let go of their children!*

And then I saw the truth: *We have more in common than I want to admit. Forgive me, dear friends, for judging you. You were in a tough place and were probably doing the only thing you knew to do.* Just as we were—doing the best we could, making terrible decisions.

Two days later, Amy and I visited the Holt adoption agency in Seoul and wrote letters to her birth mother, hoping she would look up the file. We left pictures and contact information. Amy spent several hours writing a letter to her birth mother. She had a pensive, faraway look on her face as she wrote. Later, Amy told me it was a letter of forgiveness. "I know how she feels," Amy said.

Yes, Nancy Tushabe. A lot of forgiveness.

Leaving Justice to God

Recently, a good friend and I were having lunch. A few years ago, her extended family had been ripped apart by bitter words and threatened legal action over an inheritance. I asked if there had been a resolution, any justice.

She smiled, "Actually, I'd forgotten about the incident. Things are good now between our families, and I would say the wounds are healing." She was quiet for a moment as she broke off a piece of bread. "You know," she went on to say, "I think I've learned to forget some things."

> "I know how she feels," Amy said.

Later, I thought what wisdom there was in her words. Sometimes it is good to have a "bad memory," especially when it comes to words or actions of others who have offended us. Someone once said, "Remembering is always about some degree of forgetting."

All of us have been wronged in big and small ways, and our natural tendency is to get even, to make sure someone pays. It's hard to let go because there is something in us that cries out for justice. And justice is good—there are times we must seek it, especially for those who have no voice. But justice is one thing, revenge is another. God says, "Vengeance is mine—I will repay" (Deuteronomy 32:35). For our own sakes, as well as for those around us, we must let go. God can be trusted to see that justice is done.

In John 21, Jesus is making breakfast on the seashore for His disciples after they've forsaken and denied Him. There is something healing, poignant in the gesture. It is forgiveness, but it is more than that. It is grace and mercy offered; it is grace and mercy received with humility, out of hunger and need.

Why do we resist forgiveness? We don't want to let people off the hook, maybe ourselves more than anybody. We want justice!

Jesus told us to forgive seventy times seven (Matthew 18:22). We need to keep applying the ointment of forgiveness until a stubborn wound is healed. It may take a lot of applications, but with time it will heal. We've got to just keep going there. An unknown author wrote, "Forgiveness is giving up the possibility of a better past."

> We need to keep applying the ointment of forgiveness until a stubborn wound is healed.

This morning I watched the sun come up and read the prophet's ancient words, still true today: "This I recall to my mind, therefore I have hope. Through the LORD's mercies we are not consumed, because His compassions fail not. They are new every morning; great is Your faithfulness" (Lamentations 3:21–23). Every time the sun comes up, He offers us a massive load of mercy, a fresh supply for the day!

> *Commit your way to the Lord, Trust also in Him,*
> *and He shall bring* it *to pass. He shall bring forth your*
> *righteousness as the light, and your justice as the noonday.*
> —PSALM 37:5, 6

Let Go of Bitterness

Here in the mountains of the northwest, we are vulnerable to forest fire, especially after a hot, dry summer. There's an old charred tree standing near my house, evidence that a fire swept through here once.

A few years ago, after someone had burned dead brush and tree stumps, a fire began to smolder. Our soil in central Oregon, formed of lava many years ago, in some places is so porous and rocky that the fire was actually able to burn underground. The fire came aboveground a few miles away and caused a forest fire in which several homes were destroyed, including the home of some dear friends. This raging fire, which wound its way through the root system, surprised everyone with its consuming intensity when it emerged later.

Roots are an efficient network, feeding the trees, making them grow. Some roots, especially young ones, come out easily when pulled. But then there are those stubborn ones that go deep, that hold on tight. They are the ones that have a history, that have been allowed to flourish, that have been nurtured and fed.

The more life experiences we have, the more opportunities we have for bitterness. The amazing thing is how some hurts can affect an entire life, how the bitterness can suddenly spring up, coloring everything in its path, and we wonder, *Where did that come from?*

Where Bitterness Comes From

Bitterness can come from several sources:

- *Injustice.* It can be painful to suffer unjustly at the hands of another person or organization. We believe we deserved more than what we have or that we got a raw deal. *It's just not fair!* We fume.

- *Irreconcilable loss.* Sometimes we have a hard time coming to terms with our loss. We ask, *How could such a thing happen to me?* Brad and Susan—like so many other baby boomers—are struggling to come to terms with the loss of their retirement money. Struggles like this can easily turn into bitterness.

- *Unmet expectations.* We may have had our hearts set on something, only to see our dreams evaporate. My friend Sherry fully expected to enjoy the rest of life with her husband, Steve. But he died, leaving her a young widow.

- *Unresolved anger.* Sometimes people we love or trust hurt us terribly. We feel taken advantage of, and inside we promise ourselves: "Never again will I be with those people." Bitterness takes root.

- *Disappointment in God.* We can think, *God could have prevented this from happening. And He didn't.* We feel disappointed and let down.

- *Disappointment in ourselves.* At times we mentally flog ourselves for past mistakes. If only I had done this or hadn't done that. We internalize the blame, and bitterness begins to grow.

How Bitterness Grows

Bitterness grows when it is fed. It grows when we make a home for it and welcome it into our minds and thoughts as a way of justifying our hurts. It begins with blame. We blame others, blame God, and blame ourselves. We blame organizations, and we blame the government. We get stuck in the blame, and then bitterness takes root.

> Bitterness grows when it is fed.

Bitterness is nasty stuff. Scripture talks about the power of bitterness. "Watch out that no bitter root of unbelief rises up among you, for whenever it springs up, many are corrupted by its poison" (Hebrews 12:15 NIV). How easily it can take root and spread if we allow it. Bitterness grows when we talk about the offense, when we mull it over. It grows when we get into negative patterns of thinking and rehearse: *If only they had listened to me—I was right.* Or, *He should have known better.* Or, *If she would just say she was sorry . . .* But she doesn't. He won't. And we are the ones who end up being poisoned by our own bitterness.

The Antidote for Bitterness

Jo Franz was diagnosed with MS and then, as the disease progressed, she was devastated to discover that her husband was leaving her for another woman. Jo learned the antidote to bitterness:

By forgiving those who have hurt me, I am freed from the hurt that keeps me paralyzed in a cycle that can create bitterness—churning anger that only hurts me and keeps me from being able to experience God's blessings of a new beginning. I've found that forgiveness is not only an act I must take—like saying internally or to God: "I forgive so-and-so"—but it is a process. That means whenever hurts arise through memories that are triggered so easily by a conversation, a holiday, a movie, a book, or a picture, I restate that act of "I forgive. . . ." That can literally mean years of saying those words. But I've found the process works for me, and I am able to easily pray for those people because of it. I may never know that they have taken responsibility before God, but I have that hope through prayer.[5]

Julie Wilson had to sit in a courtroom and look at her beloved mother's killer. Try telling her forgiveness is easy. It is not. C. S. Lewis wrote, "Everyone says forgiveness is a lovely idea, until they have something to forgive."[6] But the consequences of holding on to bitterness are harmful. Eventually, we must let go, or we are the ones who suffer.

> Eventually, we must let go, or we are the ones who suffer.

Walter Brueggemann said it beautifully: "Keeping kills. Relinquishing heals. . . . We do not quickly divest ourselves. But the question will have been put. . . . An invitation will have been issued. Return to the command, to the God who rests and gives rest, who sets free and satisfies. . . . We do not yield easily. But . . . if we do not yield, we shall die."[7]

A friend who was betrayed in her marriage and went through an unwanted divorce said that forgiveness finally set her free and helped to restore her life. But she said it wasn't so much a once-and-for-all gesture; it was more like shuffling steps toward forgiveness. Persistent, shuffling steps.

It is God's intention that we be healed, and He urges us, "Come to Me." To be wholly healed, we must come with our whole selves, not just our acceptable parts: "Christ says, 'Give me All. I don't want so much of your time and so much of your money and so much of your work: I want You.'"[8]

For healing to happen, we must see the truth of our experience, and invite God's presence there.

We receive healing from bitterness when we see our own sin and need for forgiveness. This awareness softens the hard ground that surrounds this stubborn root—and even when we can't deal with the root itself—and we can let God be God.

> We receive healing from bitterness when we see our own sin and need for forgiveness.

Sometimes, smoldering beneath the surface, are old wounds that cannot heal until we bring them to the surface and allow the light of God's truth to shine on them.

In writing this chapter, I've discovered an ancient wound in myself that was not healed. As I prayerfully, honestly looked at it, I asked myself, "How long am I going to hang on to this?" I realized I had maintained a sense of bitterness and hardness toward the person who caused the offense, as well as toward myself.

I "stuffed it," as they say. Like the woman who pressed through to touch Jesus, there are times when we must press through to touch Him with faith, knowing that the only true healing for our emotions is in Him. Why do we hold back? Perhaps we grow comfortable with it, thinking, *This is just the way things are.* But the truth sets us free, and for healing to begin, we must open our heart to the truth. An unhealed wound robs us of the abundant, free life and gives the wound power over us.

How do you know when an old wound hasn't healed?

- *If there's still a sting to the memory*, perhaps a sense of bitterness or a hardness about the memory, that could be an indication that you haven't healed from it.

- *If it keeps coming up*, dominating your thinking and controlling your emotion, then maybe it's still burning beneath the surface.

- *If the thought of it kills your joy* and life doesn't seem worth living anymore, that's a strong sign that an old wound needs to be dealt with.

While Joseph did not forget his several-year-old pain, he was not paralyzed by bitterness or an unforgiving attitude. If he had been, he would never have had such a useful career in Egypt. Joseph remembered, yet he was not bitter. We know he remembered, because when his brothers showed up in Egypt, he was so overcome with emotion that he had to leave the room. Seeing them brought it all back—his father, Jacob; his mother, Rachel, who died giving birth to his little brother, Benjamin. No, he didn't forget. But he did remember the God of his father who was faithful and true.

Our friends whose home was destroyed rebuilt their house on the original foundation. We, too, can be restored when our foundation is on Him. We can pray, *Be Lord of my life. All of it—every secret chamber and inner compartment. I give You my whole self and all that I have been given.* Paul the apostle said, "This one thing I do: forgetting those things that are behind, I press toward the prize" (Philippians 3:13).

With the passing of time, we must unwrap ourselves from the layers of anger and grief and sadness and despair and let new life grow, or else we can become entombed and embittered by our loss. Any kind of loss can make us bitter if we allow it. At times, life is not fair, and injustice has the potential to make us bitter. But as Dr. Richard Dobbins says, "None of us live with the facts of our lives, we live with the story we tell ourselves about those facts."[9]

> With the passing of time, we must unwrap ourselves from the layers of anger and grief and sadness and despair—and let new life grow.

As we continually apply God's truth and the balm of forgiveness to our hearts, we will feel His peace seeping into our wounds and find a joyful freedom from bitterness.

Looking carefully lest anyone fall short of the grace of God;
lest any root of bitterness springing up cause trouble, and by this
many become defiled . . . Therefore, since we are receiving a
kingdom which cannot be shaken, let us have grace.
—HEBREWS 12:15, 28A

Let Go of the Pain

I was flying home from a speaking engagement. It was a clear, crisp day, the visibility unusually good. I leaned my head against the window, drinking in the view. I was tired, and it felt good to relax. I thought of the people I had met on this trip. I had flown to a city on the other side of America where I didn't know anyone. But during a short time, I had made some new friends. One woman in particular, a leader in her community, made an impression on me. After I finished speaking, she waited until everyone else had left. Then she crumpled as she poured out her heart about the difficulties she was going through. As I listened, I was amazed again at the depth of pain in people's lives. I could tell that in spite of her outwardly put-together life, this woman was experiencing the loneliness and pain of the desert. Depression. Exhaustion. I recognized it, because I'd been there myself.

I looked out of the airplane window again. We had passed the Plains and were now over the Great Basin—mile upon mile of wilderness. It appeared to be flat, dry, and barren. What brave souls would want to live here? I wondered. And then, surprisingly, I saw little communities, a solitary house at the end of a road here and there. I wanted to shout down to them, "Hey! Why do you stay there? Don't you know that a thousand miles away are beautiful, fertile valleys where things grow? Why settle here, where you're forced to eke out an existence? You just have to get over those mountains. Get out of that wilderness!" And I'm sure many of them would shout back, "Mind your own business—we like it here. It has its own beauty, you know!"

As surely as there are times to go to the wilderness, there are also times to leave it and move on. How funny we humans are—we go kicking and screaming into the wilderness of pain or loss—and then we grow accustomed to it and resist the idea of moving on. But the time will come—if we are committed to growth—when we will let go of the pain to move on.

> Letting go of our pain means it's time to be reconciled to imperfections— ours and others'.

Letting go of our pain means it's time to be reconciled to imperfections—ours and others'. It's time to rest in unanswered questions, knowing that God is in control. Letting go means trusting that He is the perfect judge. Letting go of the wilderness means it's time to stop being a victim, time to take responsibility for where I am, who I am.

We can't move on as long as we're loaded with baggage of bitterness, regrets, and guilt. Our wonderful God says that as far as the east is from the west, that's how far He has removed our transgressions from us. When we stand cleansed in Him, He has a "bad memory" about our sins—He remembers them no more!

We can, of course, choose to stand back from God and resist being held by Him because we're angry. We can become bitter at God, which cuts us off from the very source of strength that we need. We may ask why, if God is concerned with the details of our lives, if every hair on our heads is numbered, He didn't spare us this difficulty.

If we're into the theology that God helps us find parking spaces, it can be tough to accept that a good God would not spare my house from burning when the house next door was spared. The truth is that we live in a broken world. Life happens to all of us. Some of life's difficulties come from the bad choices of others or ourselves; some hardship comes from the physical properties of our earth: sometimes fire destroys, water floods, or wind annihilates. As Scripture says, "it rains on the just and the unjust."

If we look at the life of Joseph, we see that the ingredient that made a difference in his life was his *response* to his circumstances, not the circumstances themselves. He trusted in the ultimate good plan of God.

To be held by the Father, we must let go. My friend Kathy Vick says that letting go is like being on a roller coaster. In a recent conversation I had with Kathy, she told me, "The choices we make when facing the impossible year determine who we really are and what we believe. The decision to 'let go' is really a battle cry. It says, 'I am going into this like this is just one hairy ride in my life. I will throw up my hands, scream into the sky, and lean into believing in a good God who has my back.'"

I tend to overanalyze things—to try to figure out all of life's dilemmas. But I'm growing to believe that letting go means I don't have to have the answers. Or the reasons. Or need to have it all tied up. The beauty of it is: *We can let go because we know He won't let go of us.*

A few Sundays ago, I stood in our worship service at church. Bill and I were with his elderly parents. Bill's father is ninety-seven and still prays daily for his large extended family. I held Mom Carmichael's hand with one hand and held my grandson, Hogan, in my other arm. My son Eric, and his wife, Carly, stood beside me. My husband, Bill, held their two-year-old son, Pearson, at the end of the row.

At coffee fellowship, we had just gotten hugs and kisses from Annabelle and her brother, Wesley, who go to the early service. The worship leaders were singing one of my favorite songs.

I thought of the span of the generations, the journey each of us takes through good times and hard times. I reminisced about the fresh potential of these new little ones. As I sang, I prayed for my Amy as she worked that day. I prayed that she would rest in the God who would never let her or Jeff go. I prayed for the rest of my family—my other three sons and daughters-in-law and their precious children.

Although many other things are not clear, what *is* clear is that the story for you . . . for me . . . and for all of us . . . isn't finished yet. What is clear is that God is still at work, and He holds us as we let go.

PERSONAL REFLECTION

Read the story of Joseph in Genesis, chapters 37 through 50.

1. Who do you most identify with, Jacob or Joseph? Why?
2. What attitudes of Joseph helped him succeed? Do you relate to any parts of his story?
3. Consider ways you can "forget" and be "fruitful."

Read Hebrews 12:1–2.

1. Is there something in your life that you need to "let go" to continue your journey more effectively—something that is weighing you down?
2. Prayerfully consider how you can let go.

Read Matthew 18:21–35 and ask yourself,

1. Am I holding on to a grudge or an offense?
2. Do I have one standard for others and another for myself?
3. Have I caused bitterness or resentment in anyone else?

If you are struggling with feelings of bitterness, write out the offense in detail on a piece of paper. Then pray, "Lord, I give this to You, the perfect judge. I let go of this person, this situation. I trust You with the outcome."

Find a time when you can burn this in the fireplace or otherwise destroy it. When you are tempted to relive this offense, remember that you have given it to God.

NEW BEGINNINGS RESOURCE

Moving On

As you look back over the difficult times in the past year or so, what have you learned? Prayerfully consider whether it might be time for you to move on. It may help you to record the lessons you have learned and then write some fresh, new "spiritual goals" for yourself. Put them in a sealed envelope and tuck them away somewhere to be opened and reviewed at a later date.

Recommended reading

Let Go by Fénelon
How to Forgive Ourselves—Totally by R. T. Kendall
Total Forgiveness by R. T. Kendall
Left to Tell by Immaculee Ilibagiza
My Son John by Kathi Macias (fiction dealing with forgiveness)
The God Who Won't Let Go by Dean Merrill

Trust is our gift back to God, and he finds it so enchanting that Jesus died for love of it.

—Brennan Manning, *Ruthless Trust*[1]

CHAPTER TEN

Spiritual Strategy #7: Trust God for All Seasons

A s I PUT the finishing touches on this last chapter, it is the last day of the year. What a year 2008 was! Everyone I know is relieved to have it over: job loss, stock market dive, real estate investments gone sour. The daughter of a friend of ours committed suicide. Another friend discovered he had terminal cancer. Within four months' time, friends of ours, Bonnie and Ben, both lost their fathers, and Ben was diagnosed with kidney cancer. And on and on it goes. One of my sons said, "This year really sucks." I agree.

There was good stuff, too. It just seemed harder to find the good news this year.

But when you lose a lot, you take inventory of what you *do* have: People who care. Family. Faith. A home. Purpose. The privilege to give to other people.

When all the props are kicked out from under you, you see what gets you through. And it's pretty simple: *trust*. Trust that God will see you through.

When Bill's spiritual mentor, Earl Book, was dying from heart failure, Bill visited him. Earl had just a few days to live. Bill knelt by his bed and asked, "Earl, what is God saying to you in these final hours of your life?"

This godly, learned man looked at Bill with a smile and a little twinkle in his eye. "Not one thing, Bill. . . ." He paused for a moment and said, "Except this: 'You've served Me all these years. Now . . . trust Me.'"

Nothing to Do but Trust

The thing is, we *can* trust Him. His word is good. I've seen the results of trusting him—no matter what—in my own life and in the lives of many other people. This journey we're on is actually taking us somewhere. When we trust Him, no matter what, we are transformed from being self-centered, self-absorbed, materialistic people into people of substance, who care about the big things of life, who want to make a difference and quietly determine to do just that. And we become this . . . because of what we've been through. We discover important treasures, like how much everyone needs love and encouragement. And we discover the only safe place to put our trust.

Brennan Manning tells us about the "no matter what" kind of faith.

> Unwavering trust is a rare and precious thing because it often demands a degree of courage that borders on the heroic. When the shadow of Jesus' cross falls across our lives in the form of failure, rejection, abandonment, betrayal, unemployment, loneliness, depression, the loss of a loved one; when we are deaf to everything but the shriek of our own pain; when the world around us suddenly seems a hostile, menacing place—at those times we may cry out in anguish, "How could a loving God permit this to happen?" At such moments the seeds of distrust are sown. It requires heroic courage to trust in the love of God no matter what happens to us.[2]

Sooner or later, we all encounter something bigger than ourselves. Some may find themselves facing a devastating diagnosis, like Doug and Angela received regarding their son: "How can we keep preaching the gospel when our own faith is shaken to the core?" Some are shaken, like Jim McClelland, when he went through an unwanted divorce and his whole world turned upside down. And others face a horrible ordeal, like Julie Wilson, when she experienced the trauma of her mother being murdered. But in each of these cases and many others, the victims survived—and with grace. And they have been restored. But it's the trusting in the darkest hours that got them through. What's required is a "ruthless trust," as described by Brennan Manning:

> There can be no faith without doubt, no hope without anxiety, and no trust without worry. They shadow us from dawn to dusk; indeed, they appear even in our dreams. As long as we withhold internal consent to these varied faces of fear, they are no cause for alarm, because they are not voluntary. When they threaten to consume us, we can overpower them by a simple and deliberate act of trust: "Jesus, by your grace I grow still for a moment and I hear you say, 'Courage! It's me! Don't be afraid!' I place my trust in your presence and your love. Thank you."[3]

> *I would have lost heart, unless I had believed*
> *that I would see the goodness of the LORD in the land of the living.*
> *Wait on the LORD; be of good courage,*
> *and he shall strengthen your heart.*
> *Wait, I say, on the LORD.*
> —PSALMS 27:13

Trust as a Child

Mark 10 describes a time when the Pharisees involved Jesus in a politically charged debate involving divorce. Then the parents interrupted, bringing their children to Jesus.

The disciples protested, "Get the kids out of here. They're interrupting an important discussion." But Jesus said: "No! Let them come." And then, he set a child before them and said, "Be like this."

Jesus went on to say, "I tell you as seriously as I know how that anyone who refuses to come to God as a little child will never be allowed into his kingdom" (Mark 10:15 TLB).

Jesus was teaching us to come to Him as a child, with simplicity and trust. Children can teach us a lot about trust.

Our friend Steve Savelich is a focused, take-charge kind of guy. Steve and Jan lived for a time in Salem, Oregon, and Jan worked in Portland. It was Steve's assignment to pick up their second-grade son, Jake, from school every day. One rainy afternoon Steve was working in his office, absorbed in a creative project, and he completely lost track of the time. When he glanced at his watch, he was shocked to realize he should have picked up Jake forty-five minutes earlier.

Steve hurriedly drove to the elementary school. On the way he pictured a crying, distraught little boy, wondering where his father was. When Steve pulled up to the school, all the doors were locked, the lights were out, and everyone had gone home. As Steve drove into the parking lot, there was Jake—standing beneath a tree in his yellow rain slicker holding his lunch box, swinging it back and forth. Waiting. Steve jumped out of his car, expecting to see and hear the terror he had unintentionally caused his son. "Oh, Jacob . . ." he began. "I am so sorry, son, to be so late!"

But Steve was surprised by what he saw on his son's face. There were no tears, and Jake's calm response was, "Hi, Dad! You told me you would come, so I knew you would."

Steve got in the car, and realized God was speaking to him through this incident. *Jacob trusted you and took you at your word. Shouldn't you do the same with me?*

Trusting God as a child means believing what God has said—that He will show up, He will see us through. Trusting as a child means trusting Him with a whole heart.

Each child is different, but as a rule, children are whole-hearted. They are direct. No hidden agendas, no ulterior motives, no head games, no secret sins. Children cry when they hurt, eat when they're hungry, and sleep when they're tired. When they disagree with each other, they duke it out, then let it go.

We just had the best Christmas ever with all of our children and grandchildren here at our home—that's nineteen of us, seven of them children. I must admit things got a bit chaotic at times. One night, Bill and I babysat while our sons and daughters-in-law went out for a late dinner. We thought we had the kids all asleep, but three-year-old Jackson woke up, so I lay down on the bed with him, hoping he'd go back to sleep. Instead, he was wide awake. He wanted a bedtime story, "The Twelve Bears" (a longer version than "The Three Bears"—great for stalling for more time).

Now that everyone is gone and the house is quiet, I smile as I remember those moments I had with Jackson to talk about things. It was just a lot of nonsense talk, but sweet and fun, a rare little visit.

I'm thinking that sometimes God wants to get us one-on-one, just to "talk." In your own difficult, impossible year, maybe your heavenly Father just wants to get you alone, to reassure you that He's there and that everything's going to be all right.

Trusting Him as a child means coming as you are—with your anger, frustrations, questions, and all. We can enter His presence freely, assured that we're never an interruption. His door is always open to us, no matter what's going on. To trust as a child means we can wait for Him, knowing that in His good time, He will show up.

Do you remember the fresh sense of wonder and discovery you felt as a child? You found interesting objects close to the earth: bugs, sticks, rocks, or a stray feather. You liked catching minnows in the creek.

Children see every ordinary day as wonderful. They just want to hang out with the people they love—doing ordinary things like standing at the kitchen sink, helping wash dishes. Children are optimistic, excited about today and tomorrow.

But as the years go by, things get complicated. Sometimes life just stinks. There's no other way to put it. Our dreams can be shattered. We get disappointed in people. Things happen that we never dreamed could happen. Of course, life is often wonderful, but it can also turn out to be very different from what we thought it would be. We become guarded, careful. We caution ourselves, *Not so fast with the trust. Unexpected things happen. I must stay in control.*

Delight yourself also in the LORD,
and He shall give you the desires of your heart.
Commit your way to the LORD,
Trust also in Him, and He shall bring it to pass.
—PSALM 37:4, 5

Trust Is a Choice

We treasure our independence, thinking, *I can do this; I can handle it.* And, we can! But before long, we're doing our own thing, and trusting Christ with a whole heart becomes a good idea that doesn't connect with our real lives. And we can't let go, because we think it's all up to us.

But control is an illusion. Life just happens to us, and it throws us curveballs we don't expect. However, some important things are within our control. Viktor Frankl, a holocaust survivor, wrote powerfully about it: "Everything can be taken away from a man but one thing: the last of the human freedoms—to choose one's own way."[4] We can . . .

- Choose how we respond to circumstances
- Choose our words and attitudes
- Choose to praise Him, no matter what, knowing He is in control
- Choose to do the right thing within a dilemma

Here is an acronym, TRUST, to help you remember ways to choose trust: Turn, Remember, Understand, Seek, Take."[5]

T—*Turn Away from the World*

Brad and Susan heard so much bad financial news everywhere they turned that they decided to turn off the news except for brief times. They both committed to study Bible verses that focused on faith-building messages to replace the faith-destroying news they were constantly inundated with.

We, too, can deliberately turn away from the despair and fear of the world and absorb God's strength and hope. We do that by listening to praise music or by meditating on Scripture verses that give hope and comfort. The world is relentless in its messages of fear and cynicism. We can choose to feast our minds on words of hope, faith, new possibilities, and the many blessings and opportunities we do have.

Turn off the bad news! Take breaks from the Internet. Turn away from the world so you can renew your strength.

R—*Remember God's Faithfulness*

As parents, we sometimes fail to keep the promises we make to our children. But our heavenly Father *always* keeps His promises. When we are in the midst of a trial, it's important to remember what we know about God:

- He is the same yesterday, today and forever (Hebrews 13:8).
- He is faithful, and will always do what's best and right.
- He loves us, unconditionally, forever. His Word tells us that He numbers the hairs on our head and that He takes note of every sparrow that falls, so He surely cares for us (Matthew 10:29–30).

When I am in the heat of the battle, my job is to remember that He is faithful to His promises.

U—Understand Your Limits

We do not understand many things, and we sometimes cry out, *Why me?* We certainly do not know what tomorrow holds. *If only we could see beyond today . . .* we sigh. But we can't, so we hold on to Him, knowing that God is in tomorrow and that He sees the big picture, even though we can't.

Children have total dependence on the adults in their lives. We can have that same dependence on our God. As the children's song says, "We are weak, but He is strong!" There is a humility, a submissive quality in knowing our limits and resting in Him. God shines when we are up against the impossible. Our limitations have nothing to do with God's possibilities. Jesus loves stepping in to do the impossible . . . that is where He does His best work!

> Our limitations have nothing to do with God's possibilities.

S—Seek Him First, Before and Above All Else

As children, we know who our source is—it's Mom and Dad. They know how to make things happen for us. And when we're up against impossible situations, where do we go first? When Karen and Bob's daughter was diagnosed with a serious mental illness, they knew God was their only source. Looking back at their often-confusing journey, they ask, "What would we have done without the Lord?"

Because we are God's children, God is our first line of defense, not the last resort. Trusting Him *first* is a powerful statement of faith. And the result of trusting Him is peace, knowing he will direct our paths. He who put the planets and galaxies in place holds us in His hand. Things may not look good, but when we trust Him—no matter what—we are saying, *God, You know best. I let go.*

T—Take Him at His Word

If God said it—He will do it! We may think he's late . . . but like Jake Savelich's father, He will show up. His ways are not our ways. His timing is not our timing.

Jesus fell asleep when He was in the boat with his disciples going across the Sea of Galilee. Meanwhile, a storm arose, and things didn't look so good. Terrified, the disciples woke Him up, saying, "LORD, don't you care that we perish?" (Mark 4). Sometimes it feels as if we are slugging it out down here and Jesus is asleep in our boat. Sure, He's there, but at times, it doesn't seem that He's aware of what's going on with us. It's hard to trust Him in those moments.

But He *is* there. We can wait on Him, knowing that no matter how it looks or feels, we are His children and He cares for us.

> *Fear not, for I have redeemed you;*
> *I have called you by your name. You are Mine.*
> *When you pass through the waters,*
> *I will be with you; and through the rivers,*
> *they shall not overflow you.*
> *When you walk through the fire, you shall not be burned.*
> —ISAIAH 43:1, 2

What's Your One Thing?

In the same passage where Jesus welcomed the young children, we meet another young person—the rich young ruler. He had a question for Jesus: "Good teacher, what shall I do that I may inherit eternal life?" This young man had a nagging sense that something was missing in his perfect life. Jesus said to him, "You know the commandments: 'Do not commit adultery; Do not murder; Do not steal; Do not bear false witness; Do not defraud; Honor your father and your mother.'"

The rich young ruler confidently answered, " 'Teacher, all these things I have kept from my youth.' Then Jesus, looking at him, loved him, and said to him, 'One thing you lack: Go your way, sell whatever you have and give it to the poor, and you will have treasure in heaven; and come, take up the cross, and follow Me'" (Mark 10:21).

One thing.

Jesus was basically saying to the rich young ruler, "Listen, Eagle Scout, you're hung up on 'good.' On what you can do." And then he offered him a deal: "Sell all that you have and follow Me."

And the rich young ruler said, "No deal," and turned away sorrowful, because he had many riches. He could not let go. He walked away from the loving gaze of Jesus. Then Jesus said to His disciples, "How hard it is for those who have riches to enter the kingdom of God!"

His disciples were astonished at his words. "Who then can be saved?"

Then Jesus said again, "Children, how hard it is for those who trust in riches to enter the kingdom of God" (Mark 10:13–24).

What's the "one thing" you use to get through life? The one thing that's most important, the one thing you can't let go? Whatever your "one thing" is, that one thing is where you've ultimately placed your trust.

Maybe it's a relationship that means everything to you. It may be your job or a position. It may be your abilities. It may be your financial statement. *If I mess up this one thing, I mess up big-time. I must succeed here.*

I can relate to the rich young ruler. My "one thing" has been to be a good mom. To do the parenting thing *right.* I love my children so, and I want them to have the best life possible. I pray continually for that. I tried valiantly to ensure that my children had a happy home—I'm sure all parents have the same desire. And I still knock myself out, trying to make it a reality.

When Amy and I were in Korea, one of our last stops was the orphanage where Amy had spent most of her three years before she came to us in Oregon. It had been an emotional, wonderful, difficult, and fun adventure for both of us.

Amy and I left our hotel in Seoul early Thursday morning, with an interpreter and a driver, and went to the city of Chuncheon to visit the Oh Soon Jul Baby Home. Our ultimate goal had been to find Amy's birth family. Even though we couldn't locate them at the time, we were amazed and grateful to discover their identity. But I had a growing awareness that this trip was for me, too.

I discovered that I was looking for affirmation. I wanted to be assured that I'd done good. That I'd done the right thing; that I'd given Amy a better life than she would have had without me.

As we drove into the little parking lot of what was the Baby Home, we were impressed by the new and modern building. Our guide explained to us that the old orphanage had been torn down. Now most children are kept in foster care in individual families, and orphanages are almost a thing of the past.

> I wanted to be assured that I'd done good. That I'd done the right thing; that I'd given Amy a better life than she would have had without me.

It was now a sparkling clean, well-kept day-care center. We met the attentive and capable staff. One small piece of the old building still remained. The current director explained that a lot of Korean adoptees came "home," looking for their roots, so they left part of the building standing just for them. We looked through photo albums of that time, and could see that, indeed, there have been a lot of changes in Korea in the past twenty-five years.

We sat down to visit for a few moments, and the director, through an interpreter, asked Amy if she had had a good life. I was struck by the kindness and compassion in his eyes, and I was aware that he genuinely wanted to know.

I also was interested to hear Amy's reply.

She said, "I have had a hard life. Kids at school made fun of me, made fun of my eyes. And with my learning disabilities, it has been a struggle." It was painful to hear, yet I knew it was an honest answer. It was her moment of truth, and she stepped up to it. Amy had lost a lot—her birth family, knowing who she looked like, her native language. She'd had no say in the matter. She'd just been put on a plane and flown to America to live with a frenetic mom, a busy dad, and four energetic brothers in a very Caucasian neighborhood.

Then, since she wasn't ready to parent, she'd relinquished the only flesh and blood she knew in the world when she gave up her baby daughter for adoption.

"But . . ." the director looked at me, also wanting to hear something positive. "How was your American family? Were they good to you?"

"Oh, yeah!" Amy laughed and gave me a little punch in the arm. "My mom is a little crazy, though." We all laughed, but inside, I was feeling worse by the minute.

On our drive back to our hotel in Seoul, I realized I had been expecting to be affirmed for rescuing a child out of a dire situation, for bringing her into the bosom of our family. I thought, *I've worked so hard to give her a good life. I tried my best, but instead, it seems that I added more sorrow to her life.*

I prayed silently, *Lord, now what? Where do I go from here?*

I heard a quiet, still, small voice: *Let it go. Just let it go.*

> It's arrogant to assume I can heal all my children's hurts.

At that very moment, Amy leaned over and put her head on my shoulder. "Mom, you're the best. I'm so glad you're my mom. I love you."

I said, "I love you, too, Ames." But as we made the two-hour drive back to Seoul, God did some work in me. I realized that neither what I saw at the orphanage nor Amy's response mattered. I had done the best I could, and I must leave it at that.

Now I must trust God to define success in Amy's life. He has begun a good work in her, and it is not finished. As long as we live, all of us are works in progress. We must trust Him to continue the work.

And besides, what gives me the right to have answers? Or affirmation? It's arrogant to assume I can heal all my children's hurts or that I can shield my daughter from the reality of her life. In that rather hard moment, I let go and experienced a sense of peace. I was able to let it be. Paul Tillich defines trust as "the courage to accept acceptance."[6]

As long as we hold on to the need for *our* answer, God cannot show us *His* answer. When we listen to Him in the midst of our deepest disappointments and loss, we learn wisdom. We learn things we didn't even know we needed to learn. Most of all, we learn where to put our trust.

> As long as we hold on to the need for *our* answer, God cannot show us *His* answer.

One thing. It's not so much what we do; it's where we put our trust.

Ultimately, my "one thing" must be to trust Him in all of life—in the imperfect and hard moments, as well as in the joyous and blessed moments. *Trust, no matter what.*

> *One thing I have desired of the LORD, that will I seek: That I may*
> *dwell in the house of the LORD all the days of my life. . . .*
> *For in the time of trouble He shall hide me in His pavilion;*
> *In the secret place of His tabernacle He shall hide me;*
> *He shall set me high upon a rock.*
> —PSALM 27:4, 5

Trust Him for All Seasons

I am driven frequently to the river near our home, the Metolius River. I walked there last week, and the river was running cold and clear and fast, and the trail was frozen in most places, muddy in a few spots where the sun hit. The uneven ground had patches of ice on it.

I walked carefully, trying not to slip.

The only color for miles was the reddish-orange blossoms on the wild rosebushes that line the river. But mostly the grasses and reeds along the trail this time of year are dull yellow and brown. It is still winter, after all.

A Ponderosa pine had blown down and lay over one part of the trail, and I walked around it, breaking off a branch in case I had to fend off a hungry cougar. (You never know!)

But when I looked above the cold river and the dull landscape, the towering Ponderosas and the clear blue sky sang out a promise: Soon, I'll hear a red-winged blackbird. There will be a subtle shift in the feel of the air, a taste of dirt, and the sharp, sweet smell of sap will rise up from the earth.

Seasons of Waiting

As I walked the trail, I prayed for my son, Andy. He was at that very moment having surgery to reattach a ruptured Achilles tendon. Six months, the doctor said, for him to be back to normal. Six months is a long time for a young man to wait. But he will heal, and what he will discover is that the waiting is only a season. And he will look back and remember, "It was hard. But I got through it, and I'm better now."

> Trust is often developed best when we wait.

It's hard to wait, though. It's hard to wait in the long winter days when nothing is growing, when everything is frozen.

It's hard to wait for the economy to turn around. Wait for a piece of property to sell. Wait to get that job. Wait for love to return. Wait for health to be restored. Wait for a child's behavior to improve. Wait for the awful, gut-wrenching feeling of loss to subside. Wait for good news. Perhaps you are in the long winter of waiting right now. Maybe it seems that you've hung on and hung on. Now your hands are weary from gripping. Help that had seemed imminent or promised is delayed. And you ask, *How long, O Lord, O long?*

Trust is often developed best when we wait. When Paul was in prison chained to a guard, he prayed for an open door to preach the Gospel. God answered his prayer, but probably not the way Paul expected. No doubt Paul was waiting to be released from prison in order to preach the Gospel. But Paul eventually lost his life—while he was still imprisoned. However, his writings of hope and joy from prison have reached literally millions of people throughout the centuries. Talk about open doors! (Colossians 4:24) Paul wrote: "All things work together for the good of those who trust Him" (Romans 8:28).

Walking the frozen trail by the beautiful river reminded me that the things in my life *have* worked together for good. As sure as the earth turns, a new season will come. All that I have seen helps me to trust for what I do not now see. The faithfulness of our Creator dictates the seasons. He will restore us, He will bring back the springtime. Where we are now is a precursor of what is to come.

Julian of Norwich—who lived during medieval times and was born about 1342—produced the first book written in English by a woman. Among her writings we find:

> Trust Him. Learn what it means to hide your soul in Him in this way, in utter trust. After that, your prayers will be filled with true reverence—that is, a joyful respect not mixed with resentment, demands, or bargaining. For then our natural will is to have God himself—nothing less. And God's good will is simply to have us. To wrap us in himself, and in eternal life . . . This is the sturdy foundation on which everything else in your spiritual life depends, now and forever.[7]

Seasons of Faith

Different seasons of life call for different types of faith. Of course, our trust is always in the same almighty God, but our circumstances differ from time to time. What kind of faith do you need right now for your journey?

- *Noah-type faith.* When God called Noah to build an ark, He gave Noah specific instructions on what to do: the dimensions, the materials, and why he needed to build it. God told Noah to gather the animals and that there would be a flood. Noah knew exactly what he had to do, even though it must have seemed like an enormous assignment. Noah needed big faith for a big job.

- *Job-type faith.* Job had no idea why he was going through his loss and suffering. He was not privy to the conversation between God and Satan. Job was a righteous man, and even though his friends tried to get him to repent, he knew he was right before God. He didn't know *why* he was hurting; he just knew that he was. Yet he had a stubborn faith: "Though he slay me, yet will I trust him" (Job 13:15).

With Job we declare: "He knows the way that I take; When He has tested me, I shall come forth as gold. My foot has held fast to His steps; I have kept His way and not turned aside . . . I have treasured the words of His mouth more than my necessary *food*" (Job 23:10–12).

Maybe you know exactly what your mission is—you just feel overwhelmed. Trust Him and keep going. Maybe you have no idea why you're in the place you are in, and questions hang in the air. Trust Him, my friend, knowing that He does all things well. Philip Neri, an Italian priest in the 1500s, wrote, "Cast yourself into the arms of God and be very sure that if He wants anything of you, He will fit you for the work and give you strength."[8]

Perhaps our family's story is more about getting through an impossible situation by hanging on to the daily mercies of God than it is about adoption. It's about the paradox of letting go, yet never giving up on love as we wait. It's about trusting and hoping for the best, knowing that love never fails.

Amy seems to be at peace with her choice. She and Jeff are now married; she is working again and appears to be healing. When Amy told Annabelle good-bye the other night while she was visiting our house, Annabelle gave her a big hug. Amy beamed at me, "Did you see her hug me?" It was a healing moment for my Amy. It was one of many healing moments, and I believe many more will come as the seasons unfold.

One message from God remains securely in my heart: "Trust Me. I haven't brought all of you this far to let you go." We make our plans, but ultimately, only God is in control. What we *do* have in our control is whether or not we will trust Him for rest of the journey. Two hundred years ago, the Russian monk Theophan wrote, "The principal thing is to stand before God with the mind in the heart, and to go on standing before him unceasingly day and night until the end of life."[9] And so we do.

No doubt your year has presented unique impossibilities for you. And yet our God is the God of the "possible." As He continues to write a story of love and mercy in your life, He will show you a way through, as you trust Him.

> *For You have been a shelter for me,*
> *And a strong tower from the enemy.*
> *I will abide in Your tabernacle forever;*
> *I will trust in the shelter of Your wings.*
> —PSALMS 61:3

PERSONAL REFLECTION

Read Psalm 37 and meditate on what it means to trust God. Write in your prayer journal where you can grow in trust.

1. As you look back over your own hard year, what have you discovered about trust?

2. What keeps you from trusting Him with "all your heart" right now? How can you choose to trust?

3. Think of ways you can recapture a childlike trust in your Father.

4. Are you in a place of waiting on God? Or perhaps you

are aware that He is calling you to wait on Him to teach you fresh lessons of trust. Remember that waiting on God is the most efficient use of time there is, because when we wait on Him, we adjust our hearts to His purpose. It is true that "those who wait on the LORD will find new strength. They will fly high on wings like eagles; They will run and not grow weary. They will walk and not be faint" (Isaiah 40:3, NLT).

Filling Your Heart with Trust

Trust in the Lord with all your heart, And lean not on your own understanding. In all your ways acknowledge Him, And He shall direct your paths (Proverbs 3:5–6).

As for God, His way is perfect; the word of the LORD is proven; He is a shield to all who trust Him (Psalm 18:30).

Some trust in chariots, some in horses, but we will remember the name of the LORD our God (Psalm 20:7).

In You, O Lord, I put my trust; Let me never be ashamed (Psalm 31:1).

But as for me, I trust in You, O LORD; I say, "You are my God." My times are in Your hand (Psalm 31:14a).

From the end of the earth I will cry to You, when my heart is overwhelmed; lead me to the rock that is higher than I. For You have been a shelter for me, a strong tower from the enemy. I will abide in Your tabernacle forever; I will trust in the shelter of Your wings (Psalm 61:2–4).

How to Wait on God[10]

Before you pray, bow quietly before God, and work to remember and realize who He is, how near He is, how certainly He can and will help.

Just be still before Him, and allow His Holy Spirit to waken and stir up in your soul the child-like disposition of absolute dependence and confident expectation.

Wait upon God as a Living Being, as the Living God, who notices you, and is just longing to fill you with His salvation.

Wait on God till you know you have met Him; prayer will then become so different . . . let there be intervals of silence, reverent stillness of soul, in which you yield yourself to God, in case He may have taught He wishes to teach you or to work in you.

Waiting on Him will become the most blessed part of prayer, and the blessing thus obtained will be doubly precious as the fruit of such fellowship with the Holy One.

Recommended reading

Ruthless Trust by Brennan Manning

Waiting on God by Andrew Murray

If You Want to Walk on Water, You've Got to Get out of the Boat by John Ortberg

Trusting God's People . . . Again by Blake Coffee with Debbie Taylor Williams (deals with healing wounds within the church)

The Holy Wild: Trusting the Character of God by Mark Buchanan

Notes

CHAPTER ONE: I CAN'T DO THIS

1. Madame Jeanne Guyon, *Spiritual Torrents* (Augusta, Maine: Christian Books, 1984).

2. Gail Sheehy, *Passages* (New York: Bantam, 1976), 28.

3. Arranged and paraphrased by David Hazard (Minneapolis: Bethany House, 1994), 132.

CHAPTER TWO: IT HURTS TO LOSE

1. *A Grief Observed* (New York: Bantam, 1976), 38.

2. Joan Chittister, *Scarred by Struggle, Transformed by Hope* (Grand Rapids: Eerdmans, 2003), preface, 1.

3. *Living with Your Dreams* (Wheaton, Ill.: Victor Books, 1990), 17.

4. Lewis, *Grief Observed*, 16.

5. Sherry Tucker, *Unfinished Love* (Sisters, Ore.; VMI, 2008), 303.

6. Ibid., 319.

7. Oswald Chambers, *Baffled to Fight Better* (Fort Washington, Pa.: hambers, 1931), 24.

8. A. W. Tozer, *The Knowledge of the Holy* (San Francisco: HarperSanFrancisco, 1961), 154.

9. Flora Slosson Wuellner, "When Prayer Encounters Pain," in *Weavings Reader, Living with God in the World*, John Mogabgab, ed. (Nashville: Upper Room, 1993), 87.

10. William Shakespeare, *The Merchant of Venice*, in Vol. 2, *The Complete Works of William Shakespeare* (New York: Nelson Doubleday, 1900), 331.

11. Teresa of Avila, quoted in *Doubleday Christian Quotation Collection*, Hannah Ward and Jennifer Wild, eds. (New York: Doubleday, 1998), 104.

12. Oswald Chambers, *My Utmost for His Highest* (Westwood, N.J.: Dodd, Mead, 1935), 227.

13. Dr. Bill Gaultiere, www.ChristianSoulCare.com, accessed November 12, 2008.

CHAPTER THREE: AFTER THE CARDS STOP COMING

1. Victor M. Parachin, *Healing Grief* (St. Louis, Mo.: Chalice, 2001), 69.

2. Quoted in *Mother Teresa: Come Be My Light*, Rev. Brian Kolodiejchuk, ed. (New York: Doubleday, 2007).

3. Joseph F. Schmidt, *Praying Our Experiences* (Winona, Minn.: Saint Mary's Press, 1980), 44.

4. Jonathan Swift, quoted from *Jonathan Swift: Major Works* (Oxford World Classics) (Oxford, U.K.: Oxford University Press, 2008).

5. T. S. Eliot, "The Dry Salvages," *Four Quartets* (New York: Harvest Books, 1968).

6. Robert Browning, *The Ring and the Book; Guido,* quoted in *Bartlett's Familiar Quotations,* John Bartlett and Justin Kaplan, eds. (Boston, Mass.: Little, Brown, 1992), 468.

7. Mothers Against Drunk Driving Web site, www.madd.org, accessed December 1, 2008.

8. For further information, contact www.givinghopethroughfaith.org.

9. J. W. Follette, *Broken Bread* (Springfield, Mo.: Gospel Publishing House, 1957), 33.

10. Thomas Merton, *No Man Is an Island* (San Diego: Harcourt Brace Jovanovich, 1955), 87.

11. C. S. Lewis, *Mere Christianity* (New York: Collier, 1960), 118.

12. J. R. Miller, quoted in Mrs. Charles E. Cowman, *Streams in the Desert* (Grand Rapids, Mich.: Zondervan, 1980), 79.

13. Mark Buchanan, *Things Unseen* (Sisters, Ore.: Multnomah, 2006), 29, 30.

14. See Matthew Hoffman, MD, at www.webmd.com/depression/recog nizing-depression-symptoms, accessed October 27, 2008.

CHAPTER FOUR: RELEASE THE HEALING POWER OF WORDS

1. *As I Lay Dying* (New York: Vintage Books, 1990), 53.

2. Douglas Steere, *Gleanings* (Nashville: Upper Room, 1986), 51.

3. Nancie Carmichael, *Desperate for God* (Wheaton, Ill.: Crossway, 1999), 43.

4. Quoted in Steere, *Gleanings*, 133.

5. Henri Nouwen, "God's Silence," *Seeds of Hope*, Robert Durback, ed. (New York: Bantam, 1989), 11.

6. Amy Carmichael, paraphrased in David Hazard, *You Are My Hiding Place* (Minneapolis: Bethany, 1991), 110.

7. George Herbert, Church of England clergyman and poet, 1593–1633, quoted in *The Doubleday Christian Quotation Collection*, Hannah Ward and Jennifer Wild, comps. (New York: Doubleday, 1998), 123.

8. Dean Merrill, *The God Who Won't Let Go* (Grand Rapids, Mich.: Zondervan, 1998), 23, 24.

CHAPTER FIVE: TAKE CARE OF YOURSELF

1. John Donne, *Selections from Divine Poems, Sermons, Devotions, and Prayers*, John Booty, ed. (New York: Paulist Press, 1990), 81.

2. David A. Kent and P. G. Stanwood, eds., *Selected Prose of Christina Rossetti* (New York: St. Martin's Press, 1998), 295.

3. Edward A. Taub, MD, *Balance Your Body, Balance Your Life* (New York: Pocket Books, 1999), 335.

4. Jennifer Soong, "The Debt-Stress Connection," WebMD, http://www.webmd.com/balance/features/the-debt-stress-connection, accessed November 20, 2008.

5. Victor Parachin, *Healing Grief* (St. Louis, Mo.: Chalice, 2001), 37.

6. James Blumenthal, cited in "Feel Better Faster," *The Plain Truth*, March/April 1999, 29.

7. Dr. Edmund Jacobson, quoted in Tedde Abbott, "The ABC's of Stress Management."

8. Richard Rohr, *Everything Belongs* (New York: Crossroad, 1999), 20.

9. Hans Selye, *The Stress of Life* (New York: McGraw-Hill, 1984), 433.

10. Thomas à Kempis, quoted in Charles L. Wallis, comp., *The Treasure Chest* (New York: HarperCollins, 1959), 118.

11. Susan G. Butruille, *Women's Voices from the Oregon Trail* (Boise: Tamarack Books, 1994), 123.

12. Selye, *Stress of Life*.

13. Elizabeth Somer, *The Food & Mood Cookbook* (New York: Holt 2004).

14. Ibid.

15. Taub, *Balance Your Body*, 7.

16. Jenny Stamos Kovacs, "Blissing Out: 10 Relaxation Techniques to Reduce Stress On-the-Spot," WebMD, http://www.webmd.com/balance/stress-management/features/blissin g-out-10-relaxation-techniques-reduce-stress-spot, accessed December 3, 2008.

17. Paul Tournier, MD, *Creative Suffering* (San Francisco: Harper-SanFrancisco, 1983) 49.

18. George MacDonald, quoted in *The Doubleday Christian Quotation Collection*, Hannah Ward and Jennifer Wild, eds. (New York: Doubleday, 1998), 182.

19. Susanna Wesley, quoted in *The Doubleday Christian Quotation Collection*, 156.

CHAPTER SIX: REACH OUT TO OTHER PEOPLE

1. E. Stanley Jones, *Christian Maturity* (Nashville: Abingdon Press, 1968), 31.

2. Thomas Merton, *No Man Is an Island* (New York: Harcourt Brace Jovanovich, 1955), 4.

3. See www.babynamescountry.com.

4. Henri Nouwen, *The Wounded Healer* (New York: Doubleday, 1979), 40.

5. Paul Tournier, quoted in *Embracing the Love of God* by James Bryan Smith (San Francisco: HarperSan Francisco, 1995), 146.

6. James Bryan Smith, *Embracing the Love of God* (SanFrancisco: HarperSanFrancisco, 1995), 162.

CHAPTER SEVEN: PUT ONE FOOT IN FRONT OF THE OTHER

1. John Donne, *Sermons,* John Booty, ed. (New York: Paulist Press, 1990), 208.

2. Joan Chittister, *Scarred by Struggle, Transformed by Hope* (Grand Rapids: Eerdmans, 2003), 38.

3. See "Jeanne Marie Bouvier de La Motte Guyon," *Wikipedia.org*, accessed December 10, 2008.

4. Madame Guyon, in *Experiencing the Depths of Jesus Christ,* Gene Edwards, ed. (Sargent, Ga.: SeedSowers Christian Book Publishing, 1975), 31.

5. Chittister, *Scarred*, 70.

6. *Webster's Ninth New Collegiate Dictionary* (Springfield, Mass.: Merriam-Webster, 1984).

7. Chittister, *Scarred*, 76.

CHAPTER EIGHT: SING A NEW SONG

1. John Eldredge, *Journey of Desire* (Nashville: Nelson Books, 2001), 211.

2. G. Campbell Morgan, quoted in *Treasury of the Christian Faith*, Stanley Stuber and Thomas Clark, eds. (New York Association Press, 1949), 473.

3. Ann Kaiser Stearns, *Coming Back: Rebuilding Lives After Crisis and Loss* (New York: Random House, 1988), 255.

4. Corrie ten Boom, quoted in *The Doubleday Christian Quotation Collection*, Hannah Ward and Jennifer Wild, eds. (New York: Doubleday, 1998), 247.

5. Eugene Peterson, *A Long Obedience in the Same Direction* (Chicago: Intervarsity Press, 1980), 96.

6. Henri Nouwen, *Bread for the Journey* (San Francisco: HarperSanFrancisco, 1997), 24.

7. Norman Cousins, *Anatomy of an Illness* (New York: W. W. Norton, 2005).

8. Edward King (1829–1910), quoted in *The Doubleday Christian Quotation Collection*, Hannah Ward and Jennifer Wild, eds. (New York, Doubleday, 1998), 178.

9. George MacDonald, quoted in *The Doubleday Christian Quotation Collection*, Hannah Ward and Jennifer Wild, eds. (New York: Doubleday, 1998), 182.

10. Maria Cheng, "Contagious Happiness," Associated Press, http://news.yahoo.com/2/ap/20081205.

CHAPTER NINE: LET GO, SO GOD CAN HOLD YOU CLOSE

1. Paul Tournier, *A Place for You* (New York: Harper & Row, 1968), 136.

2. Frederick Buechner, *The Sacred Journey* (New York: Harper & Row, 1982), 72.

3. C. Day Lewis, quoted in Phil Yancey, *Reaching for an Invisible God* (Grand Rapids: Zondervan, 2000), 243.

4. Rhonda Britten, Fearless Living Institute, www.FearlessLiving.org.

5. Jo Franz, *Soar Unafraid* (Mustang, Okla.: Tate, 2007), 334.

6. C. S. Lewis, quoted in *Doubleday Christian Quotation Collection*, Hannah Ward and Jennifer Wild, eds. (New York: Doubleday, 1998), 286.

7. Walter Brueggemann, *Finally Comes the Poet* (Minneapolis: Augsburg, 1989), 109.

8. C. S. Lewis, *Mere Christianity* (New York: Macmillan, 1943), 167.

9. Richard Dobbins, *Your Invisible Imprint* (Sisters, Ore.: VMI Publishers, 2001), 17.

CHAPTER TEN: TRUST GOD FOR ALL SEASONS

1. Brennan Manning, *Ruthless Trust* (New York: HarperSanFrancisco, 2000), 2.

2. Ibid., 3.

3. Ibid., 104, 105.

4. Viktor E. Frankl, *Man's Search for Meaning* (New York: Simon & Schuster, 1984).

5. Acronym developed by Steve Savelich, used by permission.

6. Paul Tillich, *The Shaking of the Foundations* (New York: Charles Scribner's Sons, 1948), 42.

7. David Hazard, *I Promise You a Crown* (Grand Rapids: Bethany House, 1995), 47.

8. Philip Neri, quoted in *The Doubleday Christian Quotation Collection*, Hannah Ward and Jennifer Wild, eds. (New York: Doubleday, 1998), 101.

9. Theophan the Recluse, quoted in *The Doubleday Christian Quotation Collection*, Hannah Ward and Jennifer Wild, eds. (New York: Doubleday, 1998), 195.

10. Andrew Murray, *Waiting on God* (Minneapolis: Bethany House, 2001).

About the Author

NANCIE CARMICHAEL AND her husband, Bill, were the founding publishers of Good Family Magazines, which included *Christian Parenting Today, Virtue,* and *Parents of Teenagers* magazines, with a combined readership of more than one million.

Nancie is the author or co-author of more than a dozen books, including: *Lord Bless My Child; Lord Bless This Marriage; Desperate for God; Praying for Rain; Selah;* and *Your Life, God's Home.* Nancie is also a frequent contributor to magazines, including regular columns in *Becoming Family* and *PE Weekly,* and is a frequent guest on radio and television talk shows.

In addition to publishing and writing, Nancie and Bill Carmichael have been teaching about relationships for more than thirty-five years. Together they frequently conduct marriage, family, parenting, and other relationship and leadership seminars across the United States and Canada. Nancie has been given an honorary doctorate recognizing her contributions to Christian publishing.

Nancie's greatest delight is her family. She and Bill have five children and seven grandchildren. They make their home in the Cascade Mountains, Oregon.

Printed in the United States
By Bookmasters